Rebecca Elena Glaser

How to Sell Dreams -

Principles of Luxury Fashion Brand Management

VDM Verlag Dr. Müller

Impressum/Imprint (nur für Deutschland/ only for Germany)

Bibliografische Information der Deutschen Nationalbibliothek: Die Deutsche Nationalbibliothek verzeichnet diese Publikation in der Deutschen Nationalbibliografie; detaillierte bibliografische Daten sind im Internet über http://dnb.d-nb.de abrufbar.

Alle in diesem Buch genannten Marken und Produktnamen unterliegen warenzeichen-, marken- oder patentrechtlichem Schutz bzw. sind Warenzeichen oder eingetragene Warenzeichen der jeweiligen Inhaber. Die Wiedergabe von Marken, Produktnamen, Gebrauchsnamen, Handelsnamen, Warenbezeichnungen u.s.w. in diesem Werk berechtigt auch ohne besondere Kennzeichnung nicht zu der Annahme, dass solche Namen im Sinne der Warenzeichen- und Markenschutzgesetzgebung als frei zu betrachten wären und daher von jedermann benutzt werden dürften.

Coverbild: www.ingimage.com

Verlag: VDM Verlag Dr. Müller Aktiengesellschaft & Co. KG
Dudweiler Landstr. 99, 66123 Saarbrücken, Deutschland
Telefon +49 681 9100-698, Telefax +49 681 9100-988
Email: info@vdm-verlag.de

Herstellung in Deutschland:
Schaltungsdienst Lange o.H.G., Berlin
Books on Demand GmbH, Norderstedt
Reha GmbH, Saarbrücken
Amazon Distribution GmbH, Leipzig
ISBN: 978-3-639-25851-6

Imprint (only for USA, GB)

Bibliographic information published by the Deutsche Nationalbibliothek: The Deutsche Nationalbibliothek lists this publication in the Deutsche Nationalbibliografie; detailed bibliographic data are available in the Internet at http://dnb.d-nb.de.

Any brand names and product names mentioned in this book are subject to trademark, brand or patent protection and are trademarks or registered trademarks of their respective holders. The use of brand names, product names, common names, trade names, product descriptions etc. even without a particular marking in this works is in no way to be construed to mean that such names may be regarded as unrestricted in respect of trademark and brand protection legislation and could thus be used by anyone.

Cover image: www.ingimage.com

Publisher: VDM Verlag Dr. Müller Aktiengesellschaft & Co. KG
Dudweiler Landstr. 99, 66123 Saarbrücken, Germany
Phone +49 681 9100-698, Fax +49 681 9100-988
Email: info@vdm-publishing.com

Printed in the U.S.A.
Printed in the U.K. by (see last page)
ISBN: 978-3-639-25851-6

How to Sell Dreams – Principles of Luxury Fashion Brand Management

Table of contents

List of figures

"People don't understand that success stems from the cohabitation of two contradictory spirits: the artist's vision and the logic of worldwide marketing." Bernard Arnault, Chairman LVMH[1]

Introduction

1.1 Relevance of the topic

Looking at the headlines in spring 2009 it was inevitable to encounter news like "Chanel sheds 200 jobs as sales of luxury items decline"[2], "Luxury retailers hit by financial crisis while discounters' sales rise"[3] or "Luxury market to contract in 2009."[4]

Maybe these headlines do not seem to be outstanding at first glance, since it became quite obvious to everybody how fatal and serious the effects of the financial crisis are and to which extent they affect the markets. However, people who are well versed about the luxury sector know that those headlines have to be taken more seriously than in any other field of business.

Among marketing specialists and industry experts luxury brands were said to be omnipotent, resistant to economic downturns and immune to financial ebbs.[5] [6] That this marketing folklore about luxury brands is not longer true can be seen by the downturn of the industry after 11/09/2001, the SARS epidemic in Asia or currently the difficulties of great luxury companies.[7] Releasing the figures of 2008, it is obvious how luxury holdings suffer. E.g. decreased the operating profit of the PPR group (holding brands like Gucci, Bottega Veneta, Yves Saint Laurent, Stella McCartney, Alexander McQueen) in 2008 about 20%. Consequently the total revenue dropped as well.[8]

According to the annual study of the consultants Bain and Company, the luxury industry faces its first recession in six years. Depicting the growth of global luxury goods sales with +6.5% in 2006 and +9% in 2007, the figure of only +3% in 2008 already shows a sharp decline, giving an indication to what will happen in 2009. The study predicts a fall of sales

---

[1] Bernard Arnault, in Levine, J. (2007). Liberté, fraternité—but to hell with égalité! In: Forbes.

[2] Davies, L. (2008), Chanel sheds 200 jobs as sales of luxury items decline. In: The Guardian.

[3] Birchall, J. (2008), Luxury retailers hit by financial crisis while discounters' sales rise. In: FT.

[4] N.N. (2008), Luxury market to contract in 2009. In: International Herald Tribune.

[5] Cp. Krauss, C. (2008), Worldwide luxury goods market growth projected to slow substantially by end of year and head into recession in 2009. In: Bain and Company Press release.

[6] Cp. Interbrand (2008), p. 2.

[7] Cp. Appendix, Interview Peter-Paul Polte, p. 67; Matthias Klein, p. 62.

[8] Cp. Lembke, J. (2009), Der Luxusmarkt hat seinen Glanz verloren. In: FAZ.

about -7% using constant exchange rates. [9] It is clear to see that the luxury fashion industry faces a challenge in the field of strategic management like never before, in order to survive those rough times.

Taking a closer look at available literature it is striking that there is only limited research about the luxury fashion industry itself and even less research about the management of luxury fashion brands. This might be due to the fact that there was a relatively slow growth in the strategic business direction. According to researchers luxury brands were for a long time managed through traditional business methods and decisions were founded on intuition and sometimes on a trial basis.[10]

As the current financial crisis shows, no brand is isolated and *managing* a luxury brand in such times is evident. However, despite the financial crisis the luxury industry held a market value of $263 billion in 2007 and has a predicted growth by 71.0% over the next five years, indicating it will hit $450 billion by 2012.[11]

As can be seen by those forecasts, there still prevails an enormous growth potential of the luxury industry, indicating that it is crucial for luxury brands to take a long-term view and business approach, making it indispensable to base management decisions on well-grounded economic theories and constructs. Taking the growth-potential and importance of the luxury industry into account, it could be expected that this market is examined and analyzed on a regular basis. However, by reviewing business press and academic papers there is only little examination of the luxury goods market and a general confusion about the subject area of managing luxury brands. The main problems are unclear parameters and a lack of definitions about what constitutes luxury goods. Furthermore the existence of numerous classical tactical action-marketing paradoxes prevails.[12]

Apparently the rapid growth of the industry, the precarious market situation and the complexity of globalization require a critical examination of luxury brand management.

Most of the existing academic papers focus on consumer behavior and attitudes towards luxury goods purchase but less on practical guidelines. The goal of this thesis is to take current social-, economic- and technical developments, as well as special features of the textile industry into account and create practicable principles for the management of luxury fashion brands. The main-part of this paper tries to examine special features of luxury fashion brand management.

---

[9] N.N. (2008), Luxury market to contract in 2009. In: International Herald Tribune.

[10] Okonkwo, U. (2007), p. 3; Dubois, B./Duquesne, P. (1993), p. 36.

[11] Verdict Research (2007), Global Luxury Retailing 2007.

[12] Renand, F. / Vickers, J. (2003), p. 3; Dubois, B./Duquesne, P. (1993), p. 43.

1.2 Procedural method

The scientific approach of this thesis is based both on comparative study of literature as well as industry expert interviews.

In a first step different concepts of *luxury* will be depicted, taking into account the etymology and history of this term, as well as new approaches of the concepts of luxury. Upon that the terms *brand, brand identity, brand image* and *brand personality* will be categorized and defined, in order to have a common understanding of terms in this paper. The next step will be bringing together the concepts of *luxury* and *brand*. The semantic field of the term *luxury brand* will be defined, adopting the concept of Dubois et alter, who assessed six main facets to define a luxury good.

Since it is pivotal to understand *why* people actually buy luxury goods, the paper proceeds illustrating economic approaches to explain the purchase of luxury goods. Since a solely socio-economic view on motives and drivers for luxury goods consumption is not sufficient to explain consumer behavior, taking socio-psychological and hedonistic approaches into account widens the concept. Since this paper deals with fashion luxury brands in particular, a short containment will be made, defining what the major luxury fashion product divisions are. In this context a closer examination of the textile industry and it is special features and dynamics will take place.

The next part of the paper comprises implications and principles for managers and creative directors in the luxury fashion industry. The aim of this part of the paper is to reveal special features of luxury fashion brand management in contrary to consumer goods. This will be carried out by means of the six Ps of the marketing mix. Convertible and evident principles for practitioners should be developed, based on the comparative study of literature. Furthermore interviews with experts from different fields of the industry were held, in order to obtain multidimensional views on the topic.

The paper closes with a short outlook on the future of the luxury fashion industry and a summary.

2 Terminologies and basic assumptions

2.1 Etymology and different concepts of the term *luxury*

Although the term *luxury* is being used widely, it is not as self-evident as it appears to be. This becomes apparent when trying to define the term luxury, which has a history of thousands of years and is even older as trade itself.[13] Kambli speaks for many ethicists, economists and sociologists when he states that no other moral or social issue is as unclear as that of luxury, and what behavior toward it can be considered to be well fit.[14]

Contemporary dictionary definitions of luxury are: 1. Something inessential but conducive to pleasure and comfort. 2. Something expensive or hard to obtain. 3. Sumptuous living or surroundings: *lives in luxury.*[15]

As can be seen, definitions of the term are often linked with normative interpretations, negative connotations and are not free of judgments. [16] The definition and concept of luxury highly depends on the century and its political, moral and economic conditions and on whom you ask. However, constantly remaining are ambivalence and complexity of consumer attitudes regarding luxury.[17]

To obtain a better understanding of the term a first step is to take an etymological approach. The word luxury has its roots in the Latin words "luxus" and "luxuria". As a general meaning of both words, the variation from the ordinary, the as normal, morally-ethical and healthy acknowledged dimension, can be stated.[18] Both "luxus" and "luxuria" have broader and more differentiated fields of meanings, however, it is hard to draw a concrete line between the two. The term "luxus" often describes an excessive way of living, referring to a wasteful handling of food (gluttony), pomp of clothes, exaggerated big and decorated buildings and voluptuousness.

"Luxuria" in contrast has a broader field of meanings than "luxus", including physically strength, opulence of arts and ebullient behavior.

It can be stated that "luxus" refers more to a description of an object or a state and is therefore static, while the term "luxuria" is more dynamic, referring to desires evoked by affects.[19]

As mentioned before, luxury was an object of attention in all centuries and always had a connotation of being against the order of a decent life.[20] However, in the course of time the perception of the concept of luxury changed and lost its reputation of being decadent,

---

[13] Cp. White, R. (2007).

[14] Cp. Kambli, C. W. (1890), in Valtin, A. (2005).

[15] N.N. (1969).

[16] Cp. Valtin, A. (2005), p. 21 f.

[17] .Cp. Dubois, B., Laurent, G., Czellar, S. (2001), p. 3.

[18] Cp. Grugel-Pannier, D. (1996), p. 17 ff; Valtin, A. (2005), p. 19 f.

[19] Cp. Grugel-Pannier, D. (1996), p. 20.

[20] Cp. Grugel-Pannier, D. (1996), p. 69.

indecent, evil and harmful. Especially with the Industrial Revolution and due to an increasing standard of living the positive aspects of luxury were emphasized.[21] A climax was reached when Bernard Mandeville's "Fable of the Bees" fueled a discussion in the 18th century about the pursuit of luxury and pride as drivers for economic success.[22]

Although nowadays luxury is still considered as something "not necessary", the definition of what *is* necessary and what *is not,* is highly individual, implicating that the concept of luxury is relatively, subjective, depending on the framework of time and place. As Coco Chanel stated it "Luxury is a necessity that begins where necessity ends."[23]

Recent discussions brought up the terms of "old or yesterday's" and "new" luxury. What that means will be shortly explained in the following.

In the 20th century the term *luxury* was mainly used to describe a product, an industry or an object. "Yesterday's" luxury was only available for the "happy few", costing a lot, exhibiting elegance and sumptuousness. The term described the lifestyle- and consumption-habits of a small elite of the society.[24] "Old" luxury was considered to be priced that only the 12% of the top earners of society could afford it, associated with iconic heritage luxury brands like Rolls Royce, Cartier or Tiffany's.[25] Danzinger sums the concept of old luxury up by stating that luxury was intrinsic to the object, and it was trough its intrinsic qualities that luxury was defined.[26]

However, lately the concept of luxury is undergoing a huge transformation referred to as the "new" luxury. There is no clear definition of the concept of "new" luxury, but it is closely linked with the phenomena of "democratization of luxury". The following part introduces a few definition approaches according to "new" luxury.

By opening up to the upper middle-class and middle-class, luxury brands became more accessible. Although compared to the mass products they are still priced at a premium level - approximately ten times higher - they are still in the financial reach of about 40% of the population.[27] Taking a closer look at today's luxury market we can observe a bisection

---

[21] Cp. Berry, C. (1994), p. 20

[22] Cp. Grugel-Pannier, D. (1996), p. 248; Mandeville, B. (1988), p. 85.

[23] Cp. Okonkwo, U. (2007), p. 7.

[24] Cp. Danzinger, P. (2005), p. 18.

[25] Cp. Saller, S. (2004); Danzinger, P. (2005).

[26] Cp. Danzinger, P. (2005), p. 20.

[27] Cp. Saller, S. (2004).

of luxury products as well as luxury consumers.[28] The David Report about "future luxury" refers to those categories as an "uber premium trend" and an "enlarged trend".[29]

According to the sociologist and professor of communication, Philippe Viallon, there are those luxury products on one side which are theoretically available for many consumers, e.g. a designer perfume, a dinner in a fancy restaurant or even a high-class watch. The second group of products, however, is still affordable for only a small elitist group at the very top of the Maslow's pyramid and unreachable for many consumers, like a yacht, a jet or haute couture fashion. Therefore, two groups of consumers can be identified. The first group is small with very high, above-average income and able to consume the luxury products from both categories. The second group is the greater mass, being able to afford luxury items from time to time, but not on a daily basis and not without thinking about the money they spend. To draw a clear distinction between the two consumer groups it can be said, that for some luxury belongs to their everyday life, whereas for the others luxury is something unique and extraordinary.[30] Although there are several approaches trying to describe the phenomena of "new" luxury, this distinction provides the basis for most of them.

It can be stated that one shift in the luxury industry is definitely the greater accessibility of luxury goods; another trend linked with the concept of "new" luxury is *experience*. According to newer research in the field of luxury consumption, luxury good consumers become more aware and experiencing overconsumption as depthless, while other aspects of life like personal development, time and wellness become more important. New luxury is more seen as an experience than material possession.[31] Recent findings of e.g. Atwal & Williams claim, that a shift of emphasis and valuation in peoples' mindsets took place, away from a transactional relationship to a holistic experience.[32] Since consumers become environmentally conscious, more educated, culturally curious, sophisticated in their taste and because time is more and more a scarce resource, the value of luxury becomes more cerebral and emotional.[33] According to that it can be said that the function of consumption shifted. Consumption nowadays has more of a social function. It is used to express one's

[28] Cp. Lipovetsky, G. (2003) in Viallon, P. (2006), p. 43.

[29] Cp. David Report (2007), p. 3.

[30] Cp. Alléres, D. (2003) in Viallon, P. (2006), p. 43.

[31] Cp. David Report (2007), p. 3.

[32] Cp. Atwal, G. / Williams, A. (2007), p. 30.

[33] Cp. Dumoulin, D. (2007); Silvertstein, M. / Fiske, N. (2008).

personality, self-fulfillment and value system.[34] Summarizing this development it can be stated that consumers became self-indulgent and pleasure-seeking individuals. Consumption plays part in expressing and creating individual abilities, finding fulfillment and developing a sense of belonging.[35] This shift suggests that the traditional conspicuous consumption approach alone is not suitable anymore to fully explain and describe consumer behavior. As Danzinger states it, the price of a product becomes increasingly unimportant to be considered a luxury. "New" luxury is more about luxury of time, space, quietness, simplicity and dreams.[36]

Taking into account all the developments mentioned above, it could rarely be seen as a coincidence that luxury brands like Armani, Bulgari, Dior and many others expanded their brands into the hotel and spa sector, which were previously "foreign territories" for them.

This diversification aims at marketing *experiences*, lifestyles and provides sensory emotional values. At top of generating experiences diversifications like the ones mentioned above enhance brad loyalty by creating synergies between meaning, perception and consumption.[37]

explore a customer profile in a survey

	Classic Status Luxury	New Luxury
Social function	Status, Prestige	Higher quality of life
Conspicious motive	Social differentiation	Individual well-being
Underlying concept	Competitiveness	Self-development
Era	Society of the masses	Society oft the individual
Objects	Cadillac, Patek, Gucci	Mass customazation
Relation to the object	Fetish	Service quality and experience
Goal in Life	More money	More time

Figure 1: Changes of the conceptions of luxury [38]

The figure below summarizes the differences between old and new conceptions of luxury. It is important to keep these trends in mind when future marketing implications in the following chapters of this paper are developed. However, as a final remark it must be said

---

[34] Cp. Valtin, A. (2005), p. 4.

[35] Cp. Atwal, G. / Williams, A. (2007), p. 30.

[36] Cp. Danzinger, P. (2007), p. 26.

[37] Cp. Atwal, G. / Williams, A. (2007).

[38] Cp. Jurik, M. (2006), Zukunftsinstitut GmbH, Der Neue Luxus.

that the concepts of "new" luxury are especially valid for mature markets like the US or most parts of Europe, while in emerging markets like China or Russia consumers still tend to prefer the "old" concepts of luxury.[39] And although there are shifts to a democratic attitude towards luxury, the principle of conveying status and distinction has not disappeared in contemporary societies.[40]

2.2 Dissociation of the terms brand, brand identity, brand image, brand personality

Since the focus of this paper lays on the marketing of luxury fashion brands, there are a few terms in this context that need to be explained and defined. Furthermore the definitions of those terms become crucial when talking about the importance of *brand loyalty* as a major principle of luxury fashion brand management.

In the following the identity-oriented marketing approach of Meffert, Burmann is adopted, since it represents one of the most recent approaches and is consistent with the basic assumptions of the marketing lectures at Zeppelin University.

The terms *brand, brand identity and brand image* are interdependent. The term brand is defined as:

> "[...] a bundle of benefits with intrinsic characteristics, differentiating itself *effectively* from another bundle of benefits, by satisfying the same basic needs, relevant to the target group."[41]

This bundle of benefits comprises *physical-functional* as well as *symbolic* components. The identity-oriented approach indicates an interaction of the *brand, the brand identity* and the *brand image*.

The *brand identity* is defined as characteristics, based on an *internal* point of view (e.g. staff, managers, owners etc.). These spatiotemporal, constant features form the character of a brand, according to an in-group.[42] According to Meffert/Burmann/Koers, *brand identity* is a self- consistent and holistic bundle of characteristics, attributes and identifiable elements that make up the brand and distinguish it on a long-term basis from other brands.[43] The *brand identity* can be also seen as a leadership concept, influencing staff´s

---

[39] "All my clients are Russian. I must educate them on the French touch though. When they first come to me, all they want is bling." Noémie Khatchadourian in: Zalkin, C. (2008), French Luxury Brands, A Modern Day Classic.

[40] Cp. Cox, B. (2008), p. 63; Appendix, Interview Matthias Klein, p. 60..

[41] Translated from Meffert, H. / Burmann, C./ Koers, M. (2005), p. 7.

[42] Cp. Meffert, H. / Burmann, C. / Kirchgeorg, M. (2008), p. 361.

[43] Cp. Meffert, H. / Burmann, C. / Koers, M. (2008); Okonkwo, U. (2007), p. 110 f.

relationships and behavior, as well as aiming at a consistent external communication about the brand's value proposition. According to Kapferer a clear *brand identity* is essential for luxury brands. Having established an identity system, it provides the basis for long-term capitalization, respect for a brand's specific itinerary and finally leads to a worldwide equalization.[44]

A wider concept of the *brand identity* comprises four dimensions; the "brand as product", "brand as symbol", "brand as organization" and "brand as person"[45] The graphic below describes the dimensions more detailed. The core of this concept builds the self-image of the brand identity.

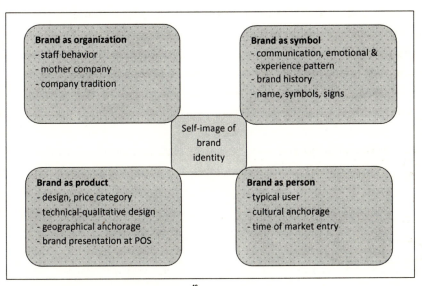

Figure 2: Dimensions of brand identity. [46]

Special about the self-image of a luxury brand is that it distinguishes itself by an *abstract-aesthetic* value proposition, whereas generic brands are characterized by a *physical-functional* value proposition.[47] The special function of the brand identity of luxury brands implies that all products under the same brand name share a symbolic identity, which characterizes and differentiates the brand through a core of specific values. Regardless of

---

[44] Cp. Kapferer, J.N. (1997), S. 259.

[45] Cp. Aaker, D. (1996), p. 78 ff.

[46] Cp. Aaker, D. (1996), p. 79.

[47] Cp. Vukelic, S. (2000) in Lasslop, I. (2002), p. 476.

the nature and the price of the product, this core of values marks the quintessence, the true self of the brand.[48]

The dimensions "brand as symbol" and "brand as product" are major determinants of the brand identity, since they hold the brand's history and the signs associated with the brand.[49] The importance of these features will be discussed more detailed in the next chapter. Regarding the brand identity it can be stated that the management has direct influence on it, whereas the brand image is not under management's direct control.

The *brand image* is defined as a constant, concentrated and judgmental image of the brand, anchored in the psyche of the relevant *external* target-group. It is the perspective how people see the brand, the way it is exposed to them. The brand image is created by the way the brand projects itself.[50] Therefore the brand image refers to an out-group. It develops and emerges over a longer period of time, due to a subjective perception of how the brand fulfills the individual needs of the customer.[51] If the brand identity and the brand image diverge, what means that the internal understanding of the brand differs from the external understanding, the brand needs to examine and realign its communication strategy in order to survive in a highly competitive market.[52]

Marketing practitioners and consumer research do not uncritically acknowledge the concept and definition of brand personality. Especially consumer neuroscience studies observed "[...] a dissociation of cortical regions subserving descriptive judgments about products and people."[53] However, the concept of brand personality is an approach that needs to be mentioned and explained in the context of luxury brands, since it is a basic assumption and crucial component of most of the theories about this topic.

The term brand personality is closely linked with the work of Jennifer Aaker, suggesting the definition of brand personality "as the set of human characteristics associated with a brand."[54] The brand personality is a component of the brand identity as well as the brand image.[55] By enduing a brand with personality traits (which are often the same as the ones of the designer / creator) it can advance to a partner in daily life. By generating additional

---

[48] Cp. Dubois, B. / Paternault, C. (1995), p. 71.

[49] Cp. Lasslop, I. in Meffert, H. / Burmann, C. / Koers, M. (2005), p. 476 f.

[50] Cp. Okonkwo, U. (2007), p. 110.

[51] Cp. Meffert, H. / Burmann, C. / Kirchgeorg, M. (2008), p. 359 f.

[52] Cp. Okonkwo, U. (2007), p. 111.

[53] Yoon, C. / Gutchess, A. / Feinberg, F. / Polk, T. (2006), p. 36.

[54] Aaker, J. (1997), p. 347.

[55] Cp. Kapferer, J.N. (1997), p. 51.

psychological benefits and emotional value, the consumer develops a relationship with the brand and identifies with it, resulting in a positive influence on demand behavior. Furthermore it is stated that the brand personality influences the perceived brand benefits, the preferences for a special brand, trust in the brand as well as brand loyalty.[56] In this context Dubois and Duquesne emphasize that an analysis of the direct relationship between consumers and brands is the key to an improved understanding of the luxury market.[57]

A clear, consistent, memorable and affirmative brand personality is important for the accurate positioning of a brand in consumer's minds.[58] The influence of the brand personality on consumer's preferences is due to the fact that human - as well as brand - personalities are defined trough values and, at the same time, signaling values. Therefore the brand personality allows the consumer to express a (desired) self-concept. Buying specific brand personalities, the consumer conveys an image to an external group, representing how he likes to see himself and how he likes to be seen.[59] This will be explained more detailed when discussing the motives why people buy luxury brands.

In the sight of all the criticism the concept of brand personality meets from neuroscientists, it is crucial to explain the symbolic functions of a brand as well as the concepts of brand relationship and brand loyalty. Although it would go beyond the scope of this paper to give detailed explanation of the concept of brand relationship,[60] the concept of brand loyalty plays an important role in luxury brand marketing and should be touched on.

In the following paper brand loyalty is defined by a *positive attitude* of the consumer towards a brand and if purchases of this brand are made *more times in a row*.[61] Brand loyalty is a conscious, as well as unconscious decision, comprising the intention to purchase as well as the continually, habitually repurchase of a specific brand.[62] [63] Furthermore a positive attitude towards the brand is significant to build brand loyalty. If the

---

[56] Cp. Büttner, M. / Huber, F. / Regier, S. / Vollhardt, K. (2006), p. 25; Meffert, H. / Burmann, C. / Kirchgeorg, M. (2008), p. 365.

[57] Dubois, B./Duquesne, P. (1993a).

[58] Cp. Okonkwo, U. (2007), p.111.

[59] Cp. Herrmann, A. / Huber, F. / Braunstein, C. (2005), p. 186.

[60] For more detailed information cp. Fournier, S. (1998).

[61] Cp. Meffert, H. / Burmann, C. / Kirchgeorg, M. (2008), p. 354.

[62] Cp. Okonkwo, U. (2007), p. 118.

[63] It must me remarked that product availability and high awareness could also be factors for repeated purchases. However, this does not mean that brands with high awareness and high sales turnover have more brand loyalty.

brand image is diffuse or if the association with the brand is negative, there is no point in buying the brand again.[64] Especially in the luxury fashion market the brand loyalty is of great importance. Since trends are changing fast, consumers might be more seduced to change their brands. Therefore, if the loyalty towards a brand is high, the consumer is more willing to follow a certain trend without changing the brand.[65] It can be stated that it should be a major goal of fashion luxury brands to build brand loyalty. Brand loyalty reduces search costs for the consumer, but more important it reduces the company's expenses for acquiring new customers (which are often four to six times higher than retaining old ones). Additionally loyal customers show less price sensitivity and purchase more frequently in higher quantities. They are willing to recommend the brand by themselves, endure waiting lists in addition to pay higher prices. Therefore loyal customers are real assets for luxury companies and it should be a prior goal for luxury fashion companies to build brand loyalty.[66] According to Okonkwo brand loyalty in the luxury fashion industry can be attained by continuous matching the consumer's taste, identification with the brand personality, satisfying service packages, reinforcing the brand presence, appealing advertisements and essence in brand message communications. In order to meet the more demanding and individualistic expectations of luxury fashion consumers, one brand is often not enough anymore to create satisfaction. Therefore a brand must create a *total* and *lasting* brand experience.[67]

2.3 Semantic field of the term luxury brand - The six main facets of a luxury good

Providing a universally valid definition of the term *luxury brand* is nearly as difficult as to define the term *luxury* itself. The following chapter presents an overview of concepts and approaches to define the term *luxury brand*.

While the term *luxury good* is used to distinguish certain product categories, the term *luxury brand* is used within a product category to label the extraordinary position of certain products within this category.

To classify luxury brands there are two general approaches, a demand- oriented and a supply-oriented. If the terms luxury good and luxury brand are used synonymously, a

---

[64] Cp. Meffert, H. / Burmann, C. / Kirchgeorg, M. (2008), p. 355.

[65] Cp. Büttner, M. / Huber, F./Regier, S. / Vollhardt, K (2006), p. 33.

[66] Cp. Okonkwo, U. (2007), p.119.

[67] Cp. Okonkwo, U. (2007), p. 120.

supply-oriented classification is implicated, depending on the product category.[68]
Therefore brands like Chanel can be, according to the product category, a unique piece of
luxury (e.g. an haute-couture dress), a luxury brand (prêt à porter fashion) or a premium
brand (perfumes, cosmetics, leather goods).[69] This hierarchical order is illustrated in the
graphic below.

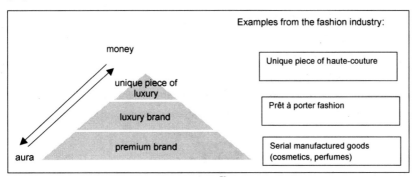

Figure 3: The hierarchy of luxury and the brand. [70]

The factors indicating the level in the hierarchy are supply-oriented, e.g. the price, the
distribution, the manufacturing process, the level of uniqueness and the product quality.[71]
While a unique piece of luxury ("*griffe*")[72] is the highest form of perfection, a luxury brand is
not a unique piece. However, it is made in small editions and also hand-manufactured in
most cases. Both, the luxury unicum and the luxury brand are located on the highest level
of quality and aesthetics. The level below comprises the premium brand, which is
produced and distributed in a higher quantity, compared to the luxury brand, and therefore
accessible for more customers. The extension of the product range, including lower-priced
items, is designed to serve as point-of-entry and generates high publicity.[73]
This concept implies that the higher levels of the pyramid (the unique pieces of luxury and
the luxury brand) have positive spillover effects on the premium brands. They convey their
special aura and image of luxury to the lower leveled premium brands, while the products

---

[68] Cp. Lasslop, I. in Meffert, H. / Burmann, C. / Koers, M. (2005), p. 473.

[69] Cp. Kapferer, J.N. (1992), p. 347.

[70] According to Kapferer, J.N. (1992), p. 352.

[71] Cp. Kapferer, J.N. (1992), p. 351 f.

[72] There is no equivalent in English, but the term basically describes a hand-made, unique piece of
an inspired creator. Cp. Kapferer, J.N. (1992), p. 348.

[73] Cp. Okonkwo, U. (2007), p. 237.

of the premium brand category generate the sales to maintain the abstract and immaterial core of the brand.[74]

However, the definition used in this paper is based on the effect-oriented perspective. Therefore a distinction between the luxury brand itself and the products being sold under the brand's name is not adopted. As already explained above (cp. brand identity), the classification is based on a holistic view, not depending on the product category, but on the abstract core of the brand.[75]

A broad empirical study of Dubois/Laurent/Czellar identified six main facets of a luxury brand, distinguishing it from other, generic brands. Although there is still no clear consensus of what constitutes a luxury brand, the facets developed by Dubois/Laurent/Czellar are considered as the most accurate global ones and used as basis in most of the literature.[76] The six facets they discovered are:

- **Very high price** (according to the absolute price (inter-categorical) as well as the price relative to other brands of the same category (intra-categorical)).
- **Excellent quality** (according to the processed materials as well as the assumed diligence of the manufacturing-process).
- **Scarcity & Uniqueness** (expressed by a difficult accessibility and rarity).
- **Aesthetics & polysensuality** (creating through design, colors etc. a value experience that touches all senses).
- **Ancestral heritage & personal history** (continuous branding in design, communications etc.).
- **Superfluousness** (dominant perception of symbolic attributes compared to technical-functional ones). [77]

Even though those characteristics are widely acknowledged in academic literature, it should be shortly mentioned that a study of Barnier and Rodina brought new findings, which should also be taken into account. The study confirmed the dimensions *excellent quality, personal history and high price* as relevant facets of a luxury good, however, it also reveals new trends in luxury goods consumption. The trend identified, amongst others, is

---

[74] Cp. Kapferer, J.N. (1992), p. 352.

[75] Cp. Lasslop, I. in Meffert, H. / Burmann, C. / Koers, M. (2005), p. 473.

[76] Cp. Vigneron, F. / Johnson, L. (2004); Barnier, V. / Rodina, I. (2006), p. 5.

[77] Cp. Dubois B. / Laurent, G. / Czellar, S. (2001), p. 8 ff.

the emergence of a "self-pleasure dimension".[78] The explanations for the emergence of this trend will be presented later in this paper when talking about consumer motivation to buy luxury brands.

Although these new findings must be mentioned, they do not touch the effect-oriented definition of luxury brands, based on the six facets developed by Dubois/Laurent/Czellar.

With the purchase and the possession of luxury goods the consumer is able to demonstrate a personal value system and the belonging to a certain social class or group.[79] All together the six characteristics mentioned above generate an *ideal benefit* for the consumer (this is also true for the new dimension of self-pleasure). Therefore Lasslop defines a luxury brand through the two categories "price" and "prevailing brand benefit".[80]

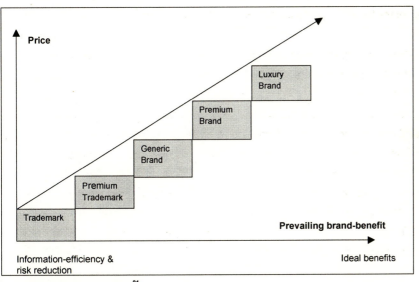

Figure 4: Brand hierarchy.[81]

According to the concept presented above, a luxury brand is a set of specific benefits, generating a highly sophisticated image in the consumer's head. The perceived benefit is primarily of an ideal nature, leading to a higher objective overall benefit of the luxury brand

---

[78] Cp. De Barnier, V. / Rodina, I. / Valette-Florence, P. (2006), p. 17.

[79] Cp. Dubois, B. / Duquesne, P. (1993), p. 43.

[80] Cp. Lasslop, I. in Meffert, H. / Burmann, C. / Koers, M. (2005), p. 475.

[81] According to Lasslop, I. in Meffert, H. / Burmann, C. / Koers, M. (2005), p. 474.

for the customer. Therefore a luxury brand creates a desire, resulting in the willingness to pay a very high price.[82]

2.4 Why do people buy luxury brands? Socio-economic and socio-psychological approaches

In order to develop principles and guidelines for luxury brand management it is crucial to understand the motives and drivers for luxury consumption. Why do people buy expensive products, which could also be purchased for a lower price with the same functional value? As already touched above, the *ideal* benefit of a luxury brand is decisive. But what exactly is the ideal benefit? This chapter aims at giving more detailed explanations for luxury brands consumption, taking into account socio-economic as well as socio-psychological approaches. Since the function of consumption has shifted (cp. chapter 2.1 Etymology and different concepts of the term *luxury) new* trends in society must be taken into account when developing an explanation approach for luxury brands consumption.

2.4.1 Socio-economic approaches

According to socio-economic approaches, luxury goods consumption has a sign value, communicating differentiation or membership.[83] The demand for luxury goods is not determined by the inherent characteristics of the goods, but by social aspects of orientation, e.g. the desire to display status or differentiate oneself from others.[84] Although the concept of *conspicuous consumption* has been addressed already in earlier times[85], the famous paper of the economist Leibenstein brought the forms of conspicuous consumption, namely the Bandwagon-, Snob- and Veblen-effect, together.[86] The purpose of conspicuous consumption is to impress others by showing what you have, what you can afford, where you belong or where you aspire to belong.[87]

The Veblen-effect implies a positive, atypical relationship between the price and the demand of a good. Hence, increasing the price of a luxury good would also increase the demand for this product, suggesting that conspicuous consumption signals wealth, and

---

[82] Cp. Lasslop, I. in Meffert, H. / Burmann, C. / Koers, M. (2005), p. 475; Valtin, A. (2005), p. 30.

[83] Cp. Cox, B. (2008), p. 49.

[84] Cp. Feemers, M. (1992), p. 108 f.

[85] Cp. Leibenstein, H. (1950), p. 184 f.

[86] Cp. Leibenstein, H. (1950), p. 189.

[87] Cp. Cox, B. (2008), p. 48.

consequently power and status.[88] Vigneron and Johnson refer to that effect as "Perceived Conspicuous Value", because publicly consumed luxury products are more likely to be conspicuous products.[89] Leibenstein divides the price of a commodity into two categories: The *real* price and the *conspicuous* price, implying that for the consumer it is only important what other individuals think the product costs (determining its conspicuous consumption utility), not what was really paid in terms of money. Therefore the price of the product could have been reduced through discounts or by the purchase in second hand stores, which would not matter in that case.[90]

The second socio-economic approach in this context is named the Snob-effect, implying a negative correlation between the market demand of a product and the individual consumer demand. Due to the fact that others are also consuming a certain commodity or increasing their consumption of that product, the snob's demand for this product decreases. This effect is explained by the wish of people to be exclusive and different from the others and the desire of disassociation from the mass.[91] Vigneron and Johnson speak of the "Perceived Unique Value", implicating that a limited supply and distribution enhances the value and preference for a brand.[92] For the so-called snobby consumer, a wider distribution diminishes the prestige value of the brand, because the status-symbolizing function vanishes.[93] The snobby consumer tries to reach distinction from other consumers by buying high priced products, which are not affordable for others with lower purchasing power.[94]

According to Leibenstein the difference between the Veblen- and the Snob-effect is that the Veblen-effect is a function of the price, while the Snob-effect is a function of the consumption.[95] However, the desired exclusiveness relating to the Snob-effect cannot be seen isolated from the price level, since a high price signalizes prestige value.[96]

---

[88] Cp. Veblen, T. (1899), p. 1 ff.

[89] Cp. Vigneron, F./Johnson, L. (1999), p. 4.

[90] Cp. Leibenstein, H. (1950), p. 203.

[91] Cp. Leibenstein, H. (1950), p. 189 ff.

[92] Cp. Vigneron, F./Johnson, L. (1999), p. 5.

[93] Cp. Adlwarth, W. (1983), p. 90.

[94] Cp. Leibenstein (1966), p. 247.

[95] Cp. Leibenstein, H. (1950), p. 189.

[96] Cp. Leibenstein (1966), p. 247; Vigneron, F. / Johnson, L. (1999), p. 6.

The last approach presented is the Bandwagon-effect, relating to a "Perceived Social Value".[97] The Bandwagon-effect states that the demand for a product increases because others are also consuming this product, implicating a positively correlated individual- and group-demand curve.[98]

Motives for such behavior are the wish for affiliation and conformity with a certain prestige group or to be distinguished from a non-prestige group. This is especially important for luxury brands, since the possession of luxury brands can be a symbolic marker of group membership.[99] Therefore Bandwagon consumers are less influenced by the price of a product as an indicator for prestige, but more by the impression they make on others while consuming specific products or brands.[100] The three effects mentioned are not necessarily solely valid for the consumption of luxury goods and with every single consumer the effects have an individual strength and composition, depending on situation and time.[101] Figure 4 below summarizes the three interpersonal effects.

As it can be seen, the consumption of luxury goods is closely linked to a social function. The next step is to present socio-psychological explanation approaches for luxury goods consumption, taking personal effects into consideration.

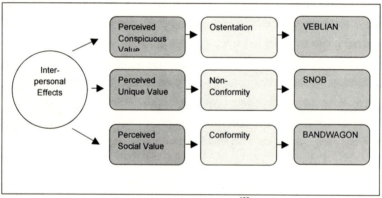

Figure 5: Inter-Personal effects on purchase behavior.[102]

[97] Cp. Vigneron, F. / Johnson, L. (1999), p. 6.

[98] Cp. Leibenstein, H. (1950), p. 189.

[99] Cp. Vigneron, F. / Johnson, L. (1999), p. 6.

[100] Cp. Vigneron, F. / Johnson, L. (1999), p. 7.

[101] Cp. Leibenstein, H. (1966), p. 247.

[102] According to Vigneron, F. / Johnson, L. (1999), p. 7.

2.4.2 Socio-psychological approaches

2.4.2.1 Self-Congruity theory

Since there are multiple socio-psychological approaches and to present them all would go beyond the scope of this paper, the following presents only a few, selected ones. A very acknowledged and important theory in this context is the *Self-Congruity Theory*. According to Rosenberg the self-concept of an individual comprises the totality of the individual's thoughts and feelings having reference to him as an object.[103] Therefore the knowledge of oneself is a system of values, attitudes, rules and goals helping the individual to organize perceptions and actions in a social context (especially family, friends and other peer-groups) and create reality of one's own. Relationships between the actions of the individual and the reactions of the environment are generated and interpreted.[104] Therefore the author of this paper defines the self-concept as the perception of an individual of the own personality, the knowledge of oneself. Newer approaches suggest the self-concept is a multi-dimensional, dynamical construct, which is shaped through an ongoing process of social experiences and is therefore individual for everyone.[105] Those multiple self-concepts can be divided into:[106]

1. The *actual self-concept,* which is the current image someone has of oneself, represents a present-component. It is primarily shaped by elements of the social identity (e.g. nationality), certain personality traits or attitudes and physical traits like hair, eye color, weight etc.

2. The *possible self-concepts* comprise a future-component of the "self". Those self-concepts generate images that are whether aspired or avoided by the individual and are therefore stimuli for future behavior. The possible self-concept has the important function of generating an assessable and interpretable context for the actual self.

3. The *ideal self-concept,* which is a special forming of the possible self-concept, meaning a desired image that someone has of oneself and exceeds the possible self-concept. It serves as a point of reference to which the individual compares the actual self. If those two concepts do not concur the individual tries to reach the ideal state.

The desire of people to express their self-concept and remain true to oneself is grounded in the *Self-Congruity Theory,* examining an individual's effort to keep a consistent self-

---

[103] Rosenberg, M. (1979), p. 9.

[104] Cp. Lasslop, I. in Meffert, H. / Burmann, C. / Koers, M. (2005), p. 478.

[105] Cp. Büttner, M. / Huber, F. / Regier, S. / Vollhardt, K. (2006), p. 36.

[106] Cp. Büttner, M. / Huber, F. / Regier, S. / Vollhardt, K (2006), p. 36 ff.

image.[107] One fundamental motive of keeping congruency is the striving for positive self-esteem. According to Rosenberg self-esteem can be defined as a positive or negative attitude towards the actual self-concept or in other words: the discrepancy between the actual and the ideal self-concept.[108]

By purchasing a famous luxury brand, which is congruent to the ideal self-concept of a consumer, self-esteem could be boosted. To clarify terms it can be stated that the motive of self-congruency is to keep a consistent factual self-concept, while a boost of the self-esteems aims at reaching the ideal self-concept.

Referring to Sirgy's *Self-Congruity Theory* consumer behavior is influenced by the comparison of one's self-concept and a brand-personality.[109] If the congruency between the brand-personality and the self-concept as well as the identification with a brand is high, self-congruency exists.[110] The consumer develops trust and close links with the brand, resulting in brand-preference and brand-loyalty.[111] Therefore a luxury brand should develop strong and distinctive brand-characteristics, helping the consumer to express his personality through the brand. The Self-Congruity Theory is one important approach to explain the consumer's motivations to buy luxury brands. However, Sirgy concedes that besides brand-personality and self-congruency other factors like functional product-attributes also influence purchase-behavior.[112]

2.4.2.2 Influence of group membership on purchase behavior

Reference groups play an important role in purchase behavior, since individuals tend to operate in a way that is consistent with the social group they identify with. Therefore those reference groups have also an influence of the products and brands an individual selects.[113] Furthermore memberships in social groups are crucial to form self-images and building self-esteem, since these feelings depend on affiliations with others and the value and significance of these emotional relationships.[114] People adopt standards from a social reference group to compare them with their own individual behavior, actions and action-

---

[107] Cp. Sirgy, M. (1985), p. 195 f.

[108] Cp. Rosenberg, M. (1979), p. 54; Büttner, M. / Huber, F. / Regier, S. / Vollhardt, K. (2006), p. 39.

[109] Cp. Sirgy et alter (1997), p. 230.

[110] Cp. Sirgy et alter (1991), p. 366 ff.

[111] Cp. Büttner, M. / Huber, F. / Regier, S. / Vollhardt, K. (2006), p. 41.

[112] Cp. Magin (2004) in Büttner, M. / Huber, F. / Regier, S. / Vollhardt, K. (2006), p. 43.

[113] Cp. Bearden, W. / Etzel, M. (1982).

[114] Cp. Fischer, R.J. (1998), p. 283.

outcomes. Therefore social reference groups serve as "comparison-platforms" and are in a normative and comparative context behavior determining.[115] While comparative reference groups are used for self-appraisal, normative reference groups function as a source of personal norms, attitudes and values.[116] Although there is no choice about certain groups we belong to because of our gender, age, race or family there are other social groups we have the option to join. Basically there are three types of influence: In case of *information-based influence* referents with high credibility and expertise serve as source for uninformed group members. Speaking of *utilitarian-influence,* group members try to comply with wishes or requirements of a reference-group to avoid punishment or receive reward. The third type of influence is *value-expressing influence*, meaning the need for psychological affiliation with the reference group.[117]

Fisher states that the loyalty to a group depends on how strong the identification with the group is. Thus, if an individual experiences the group as an extension of the self, he also experiences the successes and failures of the group on a personal level.[118]

By linking group-membership with consumption behavior it can be stated, that the degree of observation and the discussion of a purchase within the group strongly affects consumption behavior. Due to the wish for group- acknowledgment, the individual tries to impress and be consistent with the group. According to Childers and Rao publicly consumed luxury goods (like clothes, accessories, cars) are conspicuous and susceptible for peer influence, especially regarding the brand choice.[119] With the purchase of specific brands, being deemed a common icon for a social group, an individual can either strengthen the membership in this group, or try to reach membership and show congruent attitudes with a group he wished to be member in.[120] As Büttner, Huber, Regier and Vollhardt assume, a brand stands for the typical prototype of its consumer. If therefore an individual identifies with a consumer-group of a specific brand, the brand has implicit access to the individual's social identity. According to that it is spoken of an emotional relationship between a consumer and the brand as "prototypical group-member". In their study about luxury brand loyalty they found out, that the higher the social and personal

---

[115] Cp. Magin (2004) in Büttner, M. / Huber, F. / Regier, S. / Vollhardt, K. (2006), p. 51.

[116] Cp. Childers, T. / Rao, A. (1992), p. 198.

[117] Cp. Childers, T. / Rao, A. (1992), p. 199.

[118] Cp. Fischer, R. (1998), p. 283.

[119] Cp. Childers, T. / Rao, A. (1992), p. 201.

[120] Cp. Tsai, S. (2005), p. 427; Magin (2004) in Büttner, M. / Huber, F. / Regier, S. / Vollhardt, K. (2006), p. 52.

identification of an individual with a luxury brand is, the higher is the relationship quality between the individual and the luxury brand.[121]

2.4.3 Hedonistic approaches

In the context of socio-psychological approaches, the presented motives above should be replenished. Newer conceptions of luxury brand purchase by Vigneron and Johnson, Cox and Tsai suggest that the display of status, success and distinction in peer groups is not sufficient to explain the whole picture of luxury brand consumption. While the previous motives of luxury brand purchase depended on other individuals, newer approaches take personal, hedonistic motivations into account, namely *self-directed pleasure and self-gift giving*. In terms of *self-directed pleasure* consumers want to generate feelings of bliss, ecstasy and contentment for oneself. They buy a certain luxury brand for sensuous, affective gratifications, for personal development in line with their values. According to Cox, personal values are directed more inward, being about self-actualization and personal satisfaction.[122] The concept of *self-gift giving* is a form of self-communication, expressed through self-indulgence in order to satisfy one's own aspirations, fantasies or dreams.[123] A further approach developed by mood-regulation theorist Roth was the term of "affective consumption."[124] He describes the purchase of a good has the goal whether to leave a negative affective state or enter a positive affective state and develops four types of affective consumption: relief, recovery (to leave negative affective states), sensation and fulfillment (to enter positive affective states). Another purchase scenario occurs when someone wants to celebrate something for oneself and therefore indulge in a heightened emotional state. This "by the self for the self"-purpose represents one further motive of buying luxuries, in order to elicit superior feelings.[125]

Having presented socio-economic (Veblen, Snob, Bandwagon) as well as socio-psychological (self-congruency, group influence) approaches, a distinction can be drawn. The first part is the status-conveying, distinction or membership indicating function of luxury brand consumption, while the second part is the self-pleasure and indulgence seeking motivated consumption. For marketers and practitioners it is crucial to know about the different types of customers and their purchase motives, in order to develop strategies

---

[121] Cp. Büttner, M. / Huber, F. / Regier, S. / Vollhardt, K. (2006), p. 60f.

[122] Cp. Cox, B. (2008), p. 61.

[123] Cp. Mick, D.G.; DeMoss, M. (1990).

[124] Cp. Roth, G. (2001).

[125] Cp. Tsai, S. (2005), p. 428.

adopting market segmentation as well as a market positioning point of view.[126] The implications of those findings will be discussed later in this paper. The graphic below summarizes the different consumer types.

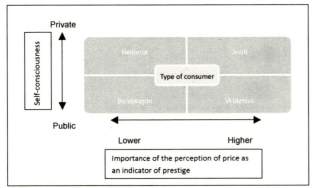

Figure 6: Different customer types.[127]

3   Features of the textile and luxury fashion industry

The purpose of this chapter is to give a short disassociation of the textile and luxury fashion industry, as well as to describe the industry structure.

The textile industry, belonging to the manufacturing industry, is closely geared with the fashion industry. Crop products like cotton, linen and sisal, animal products like wool, leather and silk or even chemical fibers are first converted into textile products (fabrics) and in a second step processed into textile commodities like bags, shoes and clothes.[128] Although most clothes are made from textiles, due to physiological, ergonomic and thermal features, not all clothes are textiles by definition.[129] However, this paper focuses only on "ready-to-wear" clothing and, according to the relatedness, on leather goods and accessories. The Major luxury fashion product divisions are presented in the figure below.

---

[126] Cp. Vigneron, F. / Johnson, L. (1999), p. 9.

[127] Cp. Cox, B (2008), p. 61.

[128] Cp. N.N. (2007), Die Textil- und Bekleidungsindustrie.

[129] Cp. Korneli, B. (2006), p. 13, Schmidt, D. (2007), p. 120.

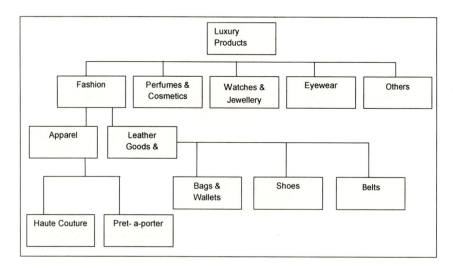

Figure 7: Major luxury fashion product divisions. [130]

During the last years an ongoing concentration in the luxury fashion market can be observed as a reaction to survive in a stringent market.[131] Due to a great wave of acquisitions, a few groups are holding a great amount of brands.[132] In terms of business volume the prime company in the luxury industry is the LVMH group with total revenue of US $6,010 million in fashion and leather goods[133], followed by PPR (Gucci group) with €3,380 million.[134] Together with Richemont these three largest companies account for some 10% of the total market, holding almost 1000 luxury brands.[135] In this context the question of a luxury brand's value arises. Since the brand is the engine of a luxury brand's business model[136], it suggests itself to measure the value of a brand, to draw comparisons between different luxury brands more easily and derive management implications. A decrease in a brand's value can be a hint for a wrong brand strategy, changing market

---

[130] Adjusted from Danzinger, P. (2007), p. 131.

[131] Cp. Bruce, M. / Kratz, C. (2007) in Hines, T. / Bruce, M. (2007), p.134.

[132] Cp. Reich, C. (2005), p. 2.

[133] Cp. LVMH (2009).

[134] Cp. PPR (2009).

[135] Cp. Bruce, M. / Kratz, C. (2007) in Hines, T. / Bruce, M. (2007), p.133.

[136] Cp. Interbrand (2008), p. 6.

demands or management failures. Therefore the brand value is an important indicator and attention must be paid to it. Namely the leading luxury brands 2008 measured by their brand value[137] are: Louis Vuitton (US $21.602 million), Gucci (US $8, 254 million) and Chanel (US $6,355 million). It is striking that all of the first three brands operate in the fashion market and have their origin in France or Italy.

One main characteristic of the luxury fashion industry are high production costs combined with short product life cycles, resulting in reduced profit margins. New products are at least generated on a twice-yearly basis with a high speed of obsolescence, demanding permanent innovations.[138]

According to a SWOT analysis undertaken by Bruce & Kratz the major *threats* in the luxury fashion industry are the dependence on political events and tourism, such as 09/11, terrorism etc., the increase of counterfeit products as well as new forms of luxury (presented in chapter 2.1). As *weaknesses* of the industry they state strong international competition (new brands), high production costs and the trend to concentration. The revealed *opportunities* are the increasing demand for luxury fashion goods from emerging countries like China and Russia as well as from younger and senior people, according to a change in lifestyles. The identified *strengths* the industry can build on are notoriety, brand values, know-how, innovation and the strict management of international channel development through selective and exclusive retailers.[139] This overview helps to gain a better understanding of the industry and the issues managers have to keep in mind when developing marketing strategies. However, the author's assumption is that this brief panorama is not sufficient to derive implications for the management of luxury fashion brands.

Therefore the next part outlines further special features of the luxury fashion industry.

Another specific feature of the luxury fashion industry is the clash of creative heads like designers on one side and business people on the other. It is a delicate balance act between creativity and commercial objectives. The Bain & Company report states that the best results can be observed in companies where big creative talents are also entrepreneurs with a market culture. This statement is also approved by the expert interviews, which can be found in the appendix of this paper. The encounter between

---

[137] Brand Value analysis according to Interbrand: Forecasted current and future revenue attributable to the brand + how does the brand influence customer's demand at the point of purchse + the brand's ability to secure ongoing customer demand (loyalty, repurchase, retention), cp. Interbrand (2008), p. 4.

[138] Cp. Bruce, M. / Kratz, C. (2007) in Hines, T. / Bruce, M. (2007), p.134.

[139] Cp. Bruce, M. / Kratz, C. (2007) in Hines, T. / Bruce, M. (2007), p.135.

creative heads and managers is a very internal and confidential issue and there is little information available about how companies deal with issues arising from that clash. However, as Ms. Seebacher-Wolf, PR Director of Strenesse International mentioned, the clash of creatives and managers is not necessarily negative, but serves as an opportunity to re-think a product or strategy.[140] Further phenomena of the luxury fashion industry are that the brand depends heavily on the sustained genius of their creator[141], or that a designer becomes the trademark of a whole brand. Famous examples in this context are Tom Ford for Gucci, Karl Lagerfeld for Chanel or John Galliano for Dior.[142] Thus design directors of famous fashion houses often attain a star-alike, elevated status. By celebrating their eccentricity in public and re-defining themselves continually the designer becomes a brand of one's own. As Anna Wintour, head of the American Vogue puts it: "There are few creative people in the fashion world who, through their spirit, their creative joy and their personalities, give fashion what it needs - some inventive madness."[143] However, if there is a strong association of a specific designer and a brand, the possible effects must be critically questioned. This strong connection could turn precarious if the designer leaves the company, or if he/she creates a special collection for another company. In order to avoid damage of the brand image and dependency on one single designer, a luxury company should invest in educating a talented community of designers.[144] Prominent examples in the context of co-branding are collaborations between top designers like Karl Lagerfeld, Stella McCartney, Viktor & Rolf or Roberto Cavalli with the Swedish fashion brand H&M.[145] Collaborations like those can be seen as a consequence of the changing environment in the fashion area. A change can be observed within both, the luxury fashion consumer and the luxury fashion brand's competitive environment. Since the consumer changed his/her interpretation of luxury fashion, it is nowadays no longer a problem to combine a €35 Zara Jeans with a €2000 Louis Vuitton bag. This change in the consumer's mindset has unconsciously built a path for mass fashion brands to stand aside luxury fashion brands. Due to their success they are no longer considered as "mass", but "mass-premium" or "high-end" brands and therefore offer alternatives to purchase luxury fashion exclusively. By adopting similar marketing and branding strategies as luxury brands (e.g.

---

[140] Cp. Appendix, Interview Brigitte Seebacher-Wolf, p. 80f.

[141] Cp. Nueno, J.L. / Quelch, J.A. (1998), p. 63.

[142] Cp. N.N. (2007), Das Designer ABC. In: FAZ.

[143] Cp. Wintour, A. in: Galliano, J. (2009).

[144] Cp. Nueno, J.L./Quelch, J.A. (1998), p. 64.

[145] Cp. Okonkwo, U. (2007), p. 227.

limited editions, high advertisement expenditure in glossy fashion magazines, celebrity product and brand endorsement, etc.) they convey a luxurious appeal. By outsourcing most of their production to Asia, mass-premium fashion brands can accomplish a fast design turnover ("fast fashion"). Consequently they impose a great pressure on luxury fashion brands to keep up with them. As a reaction, brands like Dolce & Gabbana, Prada or Chanel launching pre-collections to satisfy the consumer's needs for fast design change and early products. Although luxury fashion brands tend to adopt some fast fashion strategies to keep up with the mass-premium fashion brands, innovation and creativity should still remain the driving force for new collections.[146]

Another development in the fashion landscape affecting luxury fashion brands is the trend from "fast fashion" to "throwaway" fashion, fueled by the disposable nature of textile products. Due to a constant design-turnover and the desire to keep up-to date, fashion products become temporarily owned items, being sort out with the arrival of a new design or the emergence of a new trend. However, according to the high-prices of luxury brands, this "throwaway attitude" cannot be applied with luxury fashion products, it is simply not affordable for most consumers.[147] Therefore luxury fashion brands need to find alternatives in order to stay competitive. One solution approach is the temporarily ownership, including borrowing, exchanging and lending luxury clothes and accessories. Independent, external companies create platforms, offering services for one-day borrowing of clothes or weekly/monthly bag-rental for a subscription fee.[148] These services allow the customer to go with fashion trends and still not only purchase solely mass-premium products. However, it should be scrutinized if such services devalue the worth of a luxury brand. It could be assumed that the facet of rarity and exclusiveness diminishes, since they are accessible for a broad range of society. Yet, a refutation to this assumption could be that the *borrowing* of a luxury fashion item has not the same effect on the consumer's psyche as to *buy* a luxury item and therefore actually *owe* it.

Speaking about facets of the luxury fashion industry there is another issue that must be addressed: counterfeit luxury goods. Counterfeits are a 100 % copy of the original product intending to make the customers believe they buy the genuine product.[149] As the WTO states, international trade with counterfeit products in 2005 was estimated to be worth

---

[146] Cp. Okonkwo, U. (2007), p. 228 ff.

[147] Cp. Okonkwo, U. (2007), p. 231.

[148] Cp. Mila and Eddie (2009); Bag Borrow or Steal (2009); Albright NYC (2009).

[149] Cp. Okonkwo, U. (2007), p. 172.

$456 billion, accounting for 7% of global trade.[150] According to a study by the *National Custom Service, until 2007* counterfeiting caused a loss of 750.000 jobs in the US.[151] The major problem is that most consumers of counterfeit products do not consider the purchase or the trade with these products as a crime and are not aware of the fact, that it is a theft of intellectual property and creativity.[152] However, the big question marketers and practitioners are asking is: Do counterfeits devalue the ownership of luxury brands? In a same titled study of Nia and Zaichkowsky this issue was addressed with the result that only 25% of the respondents would buy more originals if less counterfeits were available. Another interesting result of that study was that 69% of the respondents state that the value, satisfaction and status of original luxury brands are not decreased by counterfeits.[153] Although the study result indicates that the availability of counterfeits do not significantly affect purchase behavior towards original products, it must be assumed that the image of a luxury brand could be damaged through the fact that more people possess a certain luxury brand product and therefore diminish the perceived rarity and uniqueness. Being one of the most copied luxury brands in the world, Louis Vuitton spends approximately €10-15 million every year to fight counterfeits, comprising the protection of brand rights, employing intellectual property rights specialists and agents, spotting factories and export operations of counterfeits.[154] To battle the menace, luxury fashion brand managers should concentrate on communicating the notion of exclusivity and superiority of originals, emphasizing their better quality, durability and workmanship.

4 Principles and implications to manage a fashion luxury brand

Up to now the paper outlined the different conceptions of luxury, the importance of a luxury brand's identity, image and personality, the term "luxury brand" itself, different approaches *why* consumers buy luxury brands as well as the most important features and recent development in the luxury fashion industry. Since traditional marketing approaches developed for consumer goods cannot be readily applied to fashion luxury goods, the following part of the paper focuses on developing implications and strategies for successful luxury fashion brand management. These implications are outlined by the

---

[150] Cp. Thompson, J.C. / Engle, A. / Spain, J. (2005), p. 2.

[151] Cp. United Nations Interregional Crime and Justice Research Institute Report, p. 6..

[152] Cp. Okonkwo, U. (2007), p. 175.

[153] Cp. Nia, A. / Zaichkowsky, J. (2000), p. 495.

[154] Cp. Okonkwo, U. (2007), p. 175.

means of the six marketing Ps and are based on the anthropological, sociological and historical background information examined above.

4.1 Product

4.1.1 Create experiences

On a very basic level, the product is what a consumer receives as exchange for the spent money. A product should be designed to satisfy the customer's needs. These needs comprise a functional as well as a symbolic dimension. In the case of luxury goods the symbolic dimensions plays a dominant role, since they convey an actual or ideal self-image to the public and communicate prestige, good taste and affluence. According to Okonkwo, consumers evaluate luxury goods on an abstract level and focus on non-product-related associations. In the context of luxury, however, the term product needs to be broadened: a luxury product is not only a concrete object, but always comprises a service. This could be e.g. the admittance to an exclusive club, a 24/7 available customer hotline, guarantees, free repairs, exchanges and lifetime warranties or databases documenting the customer's preferences.[155] It is therefore not exclusively the concrete product, which is in the center of the consumer's attention, but more the *experience* of luxury from a consumer's perspective.[156] This approach views the consumer not as rational-decision maker, but as an emotional-being. Since the purchase of luxury fashion products is closely linked with socio-psychological reasons and the evocation of emotions, this paper suggests an *experience-creating* marketing strategy. According to Atwal and Williams experience can be categorized into the four mutually exclusive realms: Aesthetics, entertainment, educational and escapist. Although the realms are separate, the intention is to create a "sweet spot", where the four realms meet. So how can the realms be created? The dimension of *aesthetics* comprises a total immersion in an aesthetic world, but does not require participation of the customer. This could be for example the special attention to executional details like expressive interior store design or an elevated ambience.[157] The *entertainment* aspect comprises live events where the customers absorb more than they immerse. This could be e.g. a fashion show in an art gallery or a guided tour through a design office. Again Louis Vuitton is an outrider in the field of entertainment. In 2005 the brand launched an art exhibition center called "L´Espace Louis Vuitton" within its flagship store in Paris, as a means of artistic and cultural expression. This is not only a

---

[155] Cp. Kapferer, J.N. / Bastien, V. (2009), p. 158.

[156] Cp. White, R. (2007).

[157] The retail/store design will find more attention under the chapter "Place".

source of entertainment, but also a new view on retail.[158] The challenge is to incorporate entertainment into areas that are not directly connected with the immediate experience and note they are not meant to be glamorous event-marketing initiatives.[159] The dimension *escapist* comprises active participation and immersion. By emerging into another world the customer creates new identities and realities for himself and escapes for one moment from reality. The idea of "escaping" is affirmed by the *dream value,* which is, according to Kapferer an integral part of a luxury good.[160] So how can escapism be created? One idea would be to actually create a little world or reality of its own. For example founding organizations and clubs, which are just accessible under certain conditions. Therefore not only personal escapist needs of the customer are fulfilled, but also the need for status-skills.[161] Clubs help the customer to tell a story about their purchased product and to develop networks with like-mined and like-affluent peers. One concrete example in this context is *Quintessentially,* a private members' club with a 24-hour global concierge service, and part of the world's leading luxury lifestyle group. The *Quintessentially* magazine provides (besides other services) luxury consumers with up-to-date luxury fashion and lifestyle information.[162] The last dimension *education* is the art of putting informational messages about the brand into a decorative context, so they do not appear to be educational. The consumers learn about the brand's personality through multiple channels, what is achieved by keeping consistency of design in the stores, but also through sales persons who actively live the brand. The goal is to underpin the brand promise and value by a cohesive set of positive experiences that the customer fully conceived and is able to recall.[163] The consumer needs to experience the associations with a brand and the aspirational lifestyle the brand conveys. Especially textile luxury goods are very sensory products. They are eye-pleasing designs, one can touch the noble materials, smell the fine leather etc. Therefore *experiencing* the brand is crucial in order to strengthen brand loyalty. Although the sold product stays the same, the emotions

---

[158] Cp. Okonkwo, U. (2007), p. 89.

[159] Cp. Atwal, G. / Williams, A. (2007).

[160] Cp. Kapferer, J.N. / Bastien, V. (2009), p. 160 f.

[161] "In economies that increasingly depend on (and thus value) creative thinking and acting, well-known status symbols tied to owning and consuming goods and services will find worthy competition from 'Status Skills': those skills that consumers are mastering to make the most of those same goods and services, bringing them status by being good at something, and the story telling that comes with it." Trendwatching (2006).

[162] Cp. Quintessentially (2009).

[163] Cp. Atwal, G. / Williams, A. (2007).

customers feel remain as an individual memory. This must be considered when developing a successful marketing strategy.

4.1.2 Product line management

As already traced a few times in the prior part of this paper, luxury brands face troubled times. They did not remain isolated from the financial crisis and therefore they come up with strategies in order to cut-costs or make more profit through brand extensions by reaching a broader customer base.

Bulgari e.g. adopted the first option: They left the backside of its watchbands unpolished and introduced lower-cost bottles for the perfume line.[164] It is quite obvious that this strategy is unacceptable for a company producing luxury goods, which are defined by high quality and excellence. Furthermore unconsidered short-term actions like the one above are communicated rapidly among customers and carry the danger of risking the brand's long-term value. The second option, brand extensions, in order to increase profits is a natural temptation of a luxury brand. Especially for quoted, not family owned companies the pressure of constant improvements in sales and earnings is very high, since shareholders want to leverage the value of the brand on other products in order to improve ROE.[165] The questions in this context are: To which degree is a brand extension reasonable? Where is the point the brand is attainable to so many, that it is no longer considered as a luxury and therefore loses its brand-equity?[166]

Basically there are two models of how to extent a brand: a vertical and a horizontal extension. The vertical extension creates a greater accessibility to the luxury product by bringing the absolute prize down. As shown in figure 3, this can be achieved through larger series like accessories, cosmetics and perfumes. Another model would be to extent a brand's lines. By introducing junior versions of the brand (e.g. Dolce & Gabbana's "D&G", Giorgio Armani's "Armani eXchange" or "Armani Jeans"), the brand maneuvers itself into a broader market of mainly younger customers who aspire to owe a luxury brand but still follow the newest trends.[167] These extensions remain in the same product category and therefore often profit from an already-existing know-how in this area and protect the

---

[164] Cp. Interbrand (2008), p. 1.

[165] Nueno, J.L. / Quelch, J.A. (1998), p. 62; Kapferer, J.N. / Bastien, V. (2009), p. 139; Appendix, Interview Peter-Paul Polte, p. 68.

[166] „The set of associations and behaviours on the part of the brand's consumers, channel members, and parent corporation that permits the brand to earn greater volume or greater margins than it would without the brand name and that gives the brand a strong, sustainable, and differentiated advantage over competitors." Cp. Stegemann, N. (2006), p. 58.

[167] Cp. Nueno, J.L. / Quelch, J.A. (1998), p. 65.

original brand from being overstretched. However, creativity and innovation are often compromised when moving downwards in the price pyramid.[168]

The horizontal extension is characterized by maintaining the relative prize level of the products and extent the brand in a highly coherent universe of sub-brands. These sub-brands comprise categories which have not been core categories of the brand originally, e.g. furniture, china, paintings, cafes, restaurants, hotels, spas, mobile phones, writing materials etc.[169] But what is most important: There are no inferior or superior products, there is no trading down in creativity or innovation and therefore all sub-brands are equal.[170]

Having explained the different types of brand extension the chances and risks must be outlined.

First of all a balanced product portfolio is pivotal. Most luxury fashion brands realize less than 25% of their sales from ready-to-wear fashion, whereas the rest is derived from fragrances, leather accessories and home furnishings.[171] Second, luxury brands tend to embody a lifestyle rather than a function and thus represent perfect objects to be extended. Additionally business risks can be reduced through diversification.

However, as the Interbrand Report 2008 and the interviewed industry experts put it: extensions are always a matter of "why", never of "why not".[172] The main risk of a brand extension is to comprise the brand's long-term value, the clear space it created around itself and what distinguishes it from competitors. Taking the example from figure 3, luxury consumers purchasing products from higher categories of the pyramid could be alienated, thinking that the brand's exclusivity is diminished by wider-accessible products (cp. Snob-effect). In the case of line extensions the brand could lose its appeal among the affluent customers and vice versa the appeal and share of the broader audience as well. Furthermore line extensions embody the danger of trading off the original brand or generate unprofitable cannibalization within the different lines.

By stretching the brand beyond its core-categories several risks must be considered as well. The leverage costs could exceed the profit, since the brand moves into unknown business fields where totally new skill sets are required, adding up complexity and

---

[168] Cp. Kapferer, J.N. / Bastien, V. (2009), p. 141.

[169] A shift from „fashion" to „lifestyle" can be observed, according to the emerge of new concepts of luxury (Cp. p. 8).

[170] Cp. Kapferer, J.N. / Bastien, V. (2009), p. 143f.

[171] Cp. Nueno, J.L. / Quelch, J.A. (1998), p. 64.

[172] Cp. Interbrand (2008), p. 6.

transactional costs. Especially quality control costs are a major factor, since the luxury brand has to outsource the production/service in many cases, but still maintaining high-class standard and quality. Some luxury brands try to avoid failures and embarrassment by cooperating with licensees, although there are numerous risks embedded in giving away licenses it would go beyond the scope of this paper to examine them in detail.[173] Further information about problems with licenses can be found in the expert interviews in the appendix of this paper.

In summary it can be said that luxury brand extensions should be undertaken if they contribute to the core brand image, strengthen the parent brand and reinforce the relationship between the consumers and the luxury brand. This is only possible if the brand's fashion authority and essence are transferable from the core category to the new categories. Inconsistent brand extensions lead to brand image dilution and therefore destruction of the brand's capital. Kapferer and Bastien suggest carrying out a brand core analysis before undertaking a brand extension, in order to understand the deeper meaning of the brand and if it is possible to transfer the brand image.[174] All in all brand extensions are a balance act for which it is not possible to develop a universally valid guideline. A too broad extension results in a devaluation of the brand, while a too wary extension will not be noticed and therefore does not create additional profit. Every luxury brand has to decide for itself what is its brand core and to what extent the brand image is transferable to other products. Generally it can be stated that every step towards a brand extension needs careful investigation by the management and in case an extension takes place, tight control and regulation mechanisms are crucial.

4.2 Price

4.2.1 Price–setting

Manfredo Ricca, Managing Director of Interbrand Milan stated that luxury is where demand is virtually immune to price increases.[175] This is a widely spread business bromide, implying an inelastic or even positive price elasticity. Putting it like that, the marketing implication according to the price seems to be very evident and simple: High prices, no matter what. However, reality is more complex, although luxury brands enjoy more latitude in setting the price than classic products.[176] The price management of luxury goods affords

---

[173] More detailed information in Kapferer, J.N. / Bastien, V. (2009), p. 153 ff.

[174] Cp. Kapferer, J.N. / Bastien, V. (2009), p. 146.

[175] Cp. Ricca, M. (2008), The Luxury Kingdom.

[176] Cp. Kapferer, J.N. / Bastien, V. (2009), p. 184.

painstaking control, accurate knowledge about the market situation and competitors as well as a delicate consideration of price and volume.[177]

In contrast to classic products, which are sold for their tangible, physical and utilitarian reasons, the value of luxury products derives from their intangible, ideal benefits and fulfillment of customer's "psychic" needs. Groth's marketing theory *"The Exclusive Value Principle"* states that the highest margins can be obtained by fulfilling the psychic needs of the customers. This is exactly what luxury goods do, as already explained in the previous chapters. A formula is developed, expressing the willingness to ascribe a value which is above the pure utilitarian value (PUV), therefore: Exclusive Value Premium=market value of a good/service- PUV.[178] But how to transcribe this value premium into revenue generating figures? Or in other words: How to price luxury?

Basically it can be said, that prices of luxury brands are five to ten times higher than those of premium brands.[179] In the category of luxury products the price serves as quality-indicator and a means for risk- reduction. In terms of quality- indicator expensive goods evoke an association to be better than less expensive ones whereas the dimension risk-reduction indicates the reduction of the social risk for the consumer. Since especially fashion products are displayed in public, they convey financial affluence, status and prestige and therefore reduce social risk.[180] To determine the price, a classic marketing procedure is to draw the price-consumption function and detect the price elasticity. Having a closer look at the price-volume relationship, the in chapter 3.4.1 explained Snob- and Veblen-effects can be observed. In many areas there is a positive slope of the price-consumption function, implying that price increases in this area result in higher sales, due to both, a higher margin per piece as well as higher sales volume. However, it is not the positive sloped part of the function, which determines the price, but the negative one: According to Simon and Fassnacht, that is where the optimal price is located. Hence, a luxury brand should know about its price-consumption function in order to set the right price.[181]

A further distinguishing feature of the luxury goods price policy is that prices as well as quantities are in most cases set ex ante. This procedure includes many risks: A misjudgment of the market situation can cause drastic losses in terms of money as well as

---

[177] Cp. Simon, H. / Fassnacht, M. (2006), p. 64.

[178] Cp. Groth, J. C. (1994), p. 8 f.

[179] Cp. Simon, H. / Fassnacht, M. (2006), p. 62.

[180] Cp. Lasslop, I. in Meffert, H. / Burmann, C. / Koers, M. (2005), p. 485.

[181] Cp. Simon, H. / Fassnacht, M. (2006), p. 64.

reputation and brand image.[182] Especially in the luxury fashion industry this could turn into a threat. Since styles change fast, an overproduction leads to a high rest-stock at the end of the season. The remained products run the risk to be sold through second channels for a low price, diminishing the perceived value.

Whereas classic products start with a high entry price to attract early adopters and then try to increase their number of clients by decreasing the price, luxury goods should apply exactly the opposite strategy: They start with a relatively "low" price - since the symbolic value is not known a priori - that is progressively increased in order to increase demand. This might have the effect that the luxury brand loses some customers, but since the price increase signals more value and quality, new customers can be won, who are willing to pay a higher price. Hence the price has also a sorting-out function. Of course this strategy is only applicable to a certain extent and within certain limits. If a brand moves beyond a price zone, which is considered to be legitimate for a product, it will lose customers. This price zone however starts already higher than the one for premium brands. Furthermore a price increase cannot take place over night. The first step is to come up with a product and set a price at the bottom of the zone of price legitimacy, which should be continually increased accompanied by improvements of the product. This should be practiced until the brand's optimal equilibrium zone between the price and margin.[183] But, what is most important: Luxury is not only defined through the price. If the other product facets, especially excellent quality, are not fulfilled a price increase will not work. Luxury consumers are no fools and know perfectly well what they pay and what it is worth. Thus the management implication is: If a luxury brand wants to increase the price it also has to simultaneously increase the customer's perceived value in a right proportion.[184]

4.2.2 Sales, reductions and price communication

Further matters that must be considered when developing price policy implications for fashion luxury brands are sales, price reductions and price communication.

Although fashion luxury products are liable to-as already implied by the name- *fashions*[185] and therefore underlie several changes a year, they should not be handled like any other no-name fashion item. They are still a luxury product and are therefore timeless and

---

[182] Cp. Simon, H. / Fassnacht, M. (2006), p. 65.

[183] Cp. Kapferer, J.N. / Bastien, V. (2009), p. 184.

[184] Cp. Kapferer, J.N. / Bastien, V. (2009), p. 181.

[185] „Fashion is the collective organization of programmed individual change." Kapferer, J.N./ Bastien, V. (2009), p. 189.

increase in value over time. Whereas this could be difficult when it comes to ready-to-wear fashion, leather goods and accessories should definitely fall under this definition. As already mentioned above, fashion luxury products sold for a discount price can seriously harm the brand image and should therefore never be put on sale. To give a practical example: At the end of a fashion season Louis Vuitton destroys unsold stocks rather than put them on sale.[186] This might seem uneconomic at first glance, but it is just an example that the company understood the hazardous long-term effects of short-term compromises like sales, which would cause even more losses.

Basically luxury brands have a very conservative discount policy. So what to do if a customer asks for a "price reduction"? In this case it depends heavily on the specific context and the empathy of the sales assistant. The general rule is again: Never give price advantages that could damage the brand image and the confidence in the price. The shop assistant decides which customer should benefit from special treatment. One scenario that allows a price reduction is a loyal customer, who already possesses several items of the brand, but feels guilty to buy another one. In this case a price reduction serves as a justification for themselves and their consciousness, excuse the purchase with a good bargain and a clever move. Another possible situation is the opportunity for new clients to get to know the brand and seduce them. However, the reason for the price reduction must be clearly communicated and be legitimate. Examples would be a special honeymoon offer, Valentine's Day or the obtainment of a high academic degree.[187]

The third and last matter in this context is the communication of the price. If one skips through a glossy fashion magazine it is striking that there is never a price shown in the advertisements. The reason is that there is kind of an intimate relationship between the luxury good consumer and the price. Only the one who paid for the product knows the actual price. The trick is that the presumed price of the luxury good by others should always be higher than the actual price, in order to create value and signal social distance to price-unaware outsiders.[188]

All in all, the price should remain under a mysterious aura. Therefore all communication about the price must aim at signaling the high symbolic value of the brand to justify a high price, without ever mentioning the price directly.

---

[186] Cp. Lasslop, I. in Meffert, H. / Burmann, C. / Koers, M. (2005), p. 486; Kapferer, J.N./Bastien, V. (2009), p. 189.

[187] Cp. Kapferer, J.N./Bastien, V. (2009), p. 190.

[188] Cp. Kapferer, J.N./Bastien, V. (2009), p. 70.

4.3 Place

4.3.1 Retail location & distribution channel management

The perceived rarity and an exclusive brand aura are two of the major aspects of a luxury brand. Thus, they should be lived and communicated through several channels. In this context two questions arise: Where is the optimal retail location? And second: Which channel should be chosen to distribute the fashion luxury products?

The first question is especially for luxury brands highly important. A guideline is that the location must convey the prestigious image of the brand, reinforce the core brand values, differentiate the luxury fashion brand from mass-fashion brands and also ensure commercial viability. An inappropriate retail location can harm the brand image and also the profitability, if it negatively affects the visibility, accessibility and attractiveness of the store. Therefore luxury fashion brands should position their stores in high-class districts of major capitals, in order to attract the right customer base. Other factors like human-traffic or tourist-traffic flow, population and consumer disposable income are also determining in the choice of location.[189] However, a too rapid store expansion results in brand over-exposing in one place implying that store expansions must be carefully managed. It is a balance act between augmenting the brand's visibility, brand equity and commercial feasibility as well as the costs and benefits of global expansion and growth (one sq. m. at NYC Fifth Avenue costs about €1000[190]).[191]

Accompanied is the matter of location with the question of the suitable distribution channel. Basically there are three distribution channels for luxury goods, presented in the figure below.

---

[189] In every major city a specific luxury brand retail district can be spotted, e.g. the Königsallee in Düsseldorf, Champs Elysèes in Paris, the Knightsbridge area in London, Rodeo drive in Beverly Hills (L.A.), Fifth and Madison Avenue in New York or the Quadrilatero d´Oro´ in Milan.

[190] Cp. Kemper´s (2008), Shopping auf Luxusmeilen.

[191] Cp. Okonkwo, U. (2007), p. 78f.

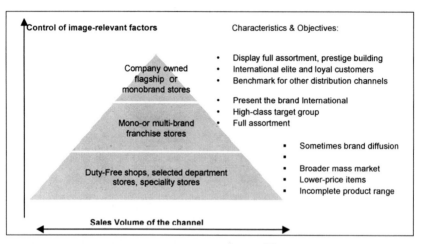

Figure 8: Distribution channel pyramid of luxury brands[192]

On the top of the pyramid is the flagship store, representing the entire brand universe in order to create a consumption experience. A common feature of flagship stores is the impressive design in terms of architecture and extravagance. Therefore it is almost a *must* for a luxury brand to have their flagship stores designed by famous architects in order to support the high-class image. Besides selling products, the flagship store has more of a psychological function. The exclusivity of the distribution reflects the exclusivity of the product and the retail experience should serve as seamless extension of the brand. A flagship store converts the intangible values of a brand into a physical manifestation by creating an excessive and exclusive consumption space. Flagship stores can furthermore serve as a market-entry strategy, communicating a brand's long-term participation and interest in the market as well as commitment to the new costumer group. However, a flagship store is accompanied with immense costs, due to astronomical occupancy- and operating-costs as well as a higher level of investment in technology and visual merchandising devices. Moore and Doherty state that only a minority of the flagship stores is profitable.[193] Despite of that, flagship stores are on the top of the distribution hierarchy, since it is the only distribution channel that enables the company to have total control over the brand in all areas, including product presentation, price, assortment as well as store atmosphere and design. In the last years a trend in the luxury fashion industry can be

---

[192] According to Lasslop, I. in Meffert, H. / Burmann, C. / Koers, M. (2005), p. 487; Nueno, J.L. / Quelch, J.A. (1998), p. 67. Adjusted by the author.

[193] Moore, C. M. / Doherty, A.M. (2007) in Hines, T./Bruce, M. (2007), p. 280 f.

observed to develop more own retail outlets.[194] Buying back franchises and licenses supports the company to have a greater secure control over the brand presentation and distribution.

On the level below the selected mono- or multi-brand franchise stores are located, according to the concept of exclusive distribution. In those stores there is whether only one brand exclusively, or more high-class brands sold. The big difference in this case is that the stores are not owned by the company, but by franchisees. The company still remains control over the brand through transparent, detailed, specific and tightly controlled distribution agreements, including prescriptions of the retail locations, merchandise-presentation and price conditions.[195] Advantages of exclusive distribution are that the economic risk is passed to the franchisee and in it is easier to enter new markets, where special know-how is required. However, the weak point of this distribution method is that it is difficult to keep the overview and control over all franchisees. Especially if it is not a mono-brand but a multi-brand store, luxury brand companies need to pay attention. Through the presentation of many brands in one store the conveying of the specific brand image of one brand could be neglected. Furthermore sales- assistants might not have the expertise and specialized knowledge of all the offered brands, resulting in bad shopping-assistance. Since they might not be familiar with all brands, they cannot justify the high prices, what leads to missed profits and damage of the brand image. Therefore the implication is that luxury brands must continuously re-check and control their distribution channels and franchisees, sorting out rigorously if brand-obligations are not fulfilled.

At the very bottom of the pyramid one can find the broadest level of distribution, including duty-frees, selected department stores (e.g. Macy's, Harrods, Bloomingdale's) and independent specialty stores. These channels are referred to as selective distribution. As can be seen from figure 8 above, this part of the distribution pyramid generates the most sales, since it offers more affordable products like perfumes, small leather goods and accessories, characterized through wide distribution and frequent purchase. The significant difference between exclusive and selective distribution is that in the latter case the brand no longer chooses its distribution network. The direct link between the customer and the brand is broken, since they are now clients of the sales point, not longer of the brand. Although this method ensures a distribution of entry-products without making them common, there are several disadvantages.[196] The limit of control is even lower here than in

---

[194] Cp. Nueno, J.L. / Quelch, J.A. (1998), p. 66; Simon, H. / Fassnacht, M. (2006), p. 67.

[195] Cp. Nueno, J.L. / Quelch, J.A. (1998), p. 67; Kapferer, J.N. / Bastien, V. (2009), p. 205.

[196] Cp. Kapferer, J.N. / Bastien, V. (2009), p. 206.

the case of exclusive distribution, often resulting in disrespect of the brand's presentation-obligations, price standards and crossing them over with premium brands. Especially with perfumes this could turn into a serious hazard, since in many duty-free zones prices are not controlled. A price spiral downward and "discounts" can be observed. How fatal this liberal price policy for luxury brands is was demonstrated in chapter 4.2.2. For the sake of completeness it must be mentioned that the Internet as a distribution channel is a controversially discussed issue in literature. However, in the context of this paper it would lead too far to carry the discussion out.[197] Detailed information about the Internet as distribution channel can be found in the interview with Brigitte Seebacher-Wolf.[198]

To draw a conclusion, the advantages and disadvantages of each distribution strategy should be shortly summarized: A solely brand-owned distribution system helps the company to keep control over the brand-code and convey the full range of the brand universe. However, this strategy generates only minor profits and appeals a smaller customer base. On the other side, multi-brand stores might be an indicator of the brand's merchandise pulling power since they are in direct competition with other brands, but also carry the danger of neglecting the brand's contract obligations.

A further disadvantage is that a mix of various channels requires separate check and control of service needs, as well as merchandise management, price policies and product lines for each channel.[199]

Concluding this chapter it can be stated that the right distribution strategy is crucial to increase profits, competitiveness and customer loyalty. Therefore a luxury brand must continually analyze its sales figures, customer satisfaction and coherence with the brand image of each channel, to develop the perfect distribution strategy. In the case of a franchise system, tight control and periodical checks of the retail locations are crucial in order to maintain a high brand value and stay competitive.

4.4 Promotion

Promotion in the luxury fashion industry is a complex marketing task, or to be more precise: it is could be seen as a paradox. The paradox is that as many consumers as possible should be persuaded that they are buying a highly exclusive luxury good. Simultaneously, the promotion needs to conceal the fact that with rising sales the product

---

[197] More detailed information in Kapferer, J.N. / Bastien, V. (2009), p. 207 ff.; Moore, C. M. / Doherty, A.M. in Hines, T. / Bruce, M. (2007), p. 240 f.; Okonkwo, U. (2007), p. 178 f. Amongst others.

[198] Cp. Appendix, Interview Brigitte Seebacher-Wolf, p. 78 f.

[199] Cp. Nueno, J.L. / Quelch, J.A. (1998), p. 68.

loses its exclusivity.[200] This turns out to be especially difficult nowadays, since companies must disclose their sales figures. The question arises, if the notion of *widely sold luxury goods* is not an oxymoron.[201] Therefore the big challenge in luxury fashion brand promotion is to deliver the consumers an illusion of rarity of products, which are objectively not limited. Thus, luxury brands have to convey the brand's exclusiveness and essence as well as the desired brand image in all sorts of communication, and what is most important: choose the appropriate promotional medium for the message. According to literature, the three most effective and suitable promotional mediums for luxury brands are: advertising, public relations and sponsorships.[202]

4.4.1 Advertising

The advertisement budget of luxury fashion brands is usually 5-15% of the revenue, including public relations and sponsorships even 25%.[203] Since luxury fashion brands target at an only small group of society, the major part of this budget is traditionally invested in advertising campaigns featured in glossy, selected, high-end publications like fashion-, business- and airline-magazines, which complement and enhance the prestige nature of luxury goods.[204] Although these publications are also read by a larger group of people who cannot afford the luxury fashion product, it serves to increase the brand awareness. In order to develop a successful advertising campaign one must consider the special features of the luxury fashion product. First and foremost not the product's tangible features should be promoted. Examining the advertisements of luxury fashion products it is striking that the element of speech is often equal zero. This can be explained that it is rather the dream, the lifestyle and the symbolic value associated with the brand that should be communicated, instead of the tangible and functional features like it is applied with consumer goods. The trick is not to show the reality, but to evoke desire and lust, propelling consumers to seek luxury goods.[205]

Therefore some implications can be derived, in order to create a credible advertisement campaign with positive long-term effects on the brand image. One important aspect is to

---

[200] Cp. Viallon, P. (2006), p. 44.

[201] Cp. Catry, B. (2003), p. 11.

[202] Cp. Kapferer, J.N. / Bastien, V. (2009), p. 210 ff.; Okonkwo, U. (2007), p. 144 ff.; Lasslop, I. in Meffert, H. / Burmann, C. / Koers, M. (2005), p. 488.

[203] Cp. Okonkwo, U. (2007), p. 145.

[204] TV advertisement has no filter criteria at all. Therefore little attention is paid to this medium. Exceptions are perfume advertisements, since they target at a broader market.

[205] Cp. Okonkwo, U. (2007), p. 152.

maintain coherence in the used symbols and codes. The eye-catcher and therefore most important symbol for a luxury fashion brand is the brand logo, often consisting out of the brand's initials in a specific type of writing (e.g. Chanel's double C or Louis Vuitton's monogram canvas) and a logotype image, like Versace's medusa head or Hermes´ horse-drawn carriage. Furthermore specific brand colors should be a consistent part of advertisements over time. Maintaining coherence in these fields is pivotal, since it encourages a higher recognition-value and therefore sticks more easily in the customer's memory. In addition to a brand logo the advertisement should convey the specific characteristics of a fashion luxury brand; namely origin, high quality, know-how, history and heritage, in order to emphasize credibility. This can be implemented by communicating the founding year (since…), the location of origin (often France or Italy), by displaying the signature of the brand's creator or through close-ups of precise manufacturing details. Although these general rules may seem easily to fulfill, it is not enough for a luxury fashion brand to survive in a highly competitive market. Likewise in all other markets, a brand must differentiate itself from its competitors also through the advertisement. According to Okonkwo, the problem is that luxury fashion brands *do* have differing underlying personalities, but their advertising messages often reflect the same brand image and personality.[206] This could be avoided by focusing more on brand innovations and re-inventions, the audacity to go new ways without compromising the brand's essence, but also the consideration of customer's preferences and expectations.

Furthermore the integration of celebrities is widely used, but also critical discussed question in marketing literature about luxury fashion brands. There are various forms of integration like celebrity brand-ambassadors, testimonials, or product placement in movies. It would go beyond the scope of this paper to elaborate this discussion. What can be recorded is that when a celebrity endorsement is applied, several things must be checked: The celebrity must have credibility and talent in their field of activity, global and constant appeal, a brand-matching personality and it must be reassured that the brand and the celebrity have uniform power, in order to avoid mutual outshine-effects.[207] Celebrity endorsement calls for clear selection criteria, since there are also numerous dangers inter-connected with this strategy: Many stars have a 24/7 media attention which makes it easy for them to get involved in public controversies according their private or professional life. This could damage the celebrity's image and vice versa also the brand image. Further hazards are if the star suddenly decides to change her/his image in a non-

---

[206] Cp. Okonkwo, U. (2007), p. 149.

[207] Cp. Okonkwo, U. (2007), p. 161.

suitable way for the brand or if they lose their shine and fall out of fashion, even before the campaign started. Celebrity endorsement can also carry great advantages, like positioning or re-positioning a brand, sustaining a brand aura, vitalize or revitalize a brand or reach a global market. [208] But this is only possible if the celebrity matches the brand and if the brand does not rely on a celebrity's appeal but already has an effective business strategy and well-defined personality.

Finally it can be stated that all advertisement activities need to keep balance between the emphasis of the creative leader, the brand logo and the design output - the product itself - as well as contribute to the desired brand image. [209]

4.4.2 Public relations & sponsorships

Public Relations play a crucial role in the promotion strategy of a luxury fashion brand, since their messages are often more credible than paid advertisement campaigns. They are designed to reinforce a brand's authenticity, prestige, identity and image, but also to maintain the goodwill of consumers, stakeholders and competitors as well as to extent press coverage. Basically public relations aim at communicating to a smaller, more selected audience and create excitement, risk and emotions while on the contrary advertisement brings assurance to the customer. [210] By creating an experience and a buzz around a brand or product, public relation events often leave a long-lasting impression in people's mind. Hence the luxury brand is challenged to maintain positive associations at all times. This becomes even more important when considering the word-of-mouth publicity PR activities jolt. Taking furthermore into account the shifts in consumer's luxury conception[211], a public relations strategy must know *who* the brand's customers are and *what* they expect from the brand. Besides glamorous staged events like fashion shows or product launches, a trend to more "good deeds" can be observed in the PR activities of fashion luxury brands. These activities include humanitarian help like supporting anti-AIDS foundations, funds for handicapped people, fighting breast cancer but also environmental and cultural projects like anti-fur movements, lobbying governments to fight counterfeits as well as promoting different art projects. [212] An implication can be stated that not every PR activity works with every brand. The chosen PR activity must be coherent with the brand

---

[208] Cp. Okonkwo, U. (2007), p. 156 ff.

[209] Cp. Nueno, J.L. / Quelch, J.A. (1998), p. 64.

[210] Cp. Catry, B. (2003), p. 15.

[211] E.g. more ethical, cultural and environmental awareness, seeking more substance and depth in luxury consumption. Cp. Chapter 2.1.

[212] Cp. Okonkwo, U. (2007), p. 155.

strategy, the brand image and the target-audience's expectations as well as it must generate a distinctive and innovative surplus for the brand.

Sponsorships have basically the same objectives as public relation activities and thus can be considered as an extension of them. By supporting a prestigious event financially, the brand can profit from positive association with the event and generates, in the best case, brand loyalty among the participants who have enjoyed the event. Furthermore sponsorship activities usually target a very specific market segment and if the right event is chosen, luxury brands can gain access to some of the world wealthiest people.[213] Examples would be prestigious sport events, e.g. golf cups, sailing regattas etc., art exhibitions and charity events. However, the same rules as with PR activities must be applied in the case of sponsorships: Coherence with the unique essence of the brand must be ensured and continuously re-checked. Additionally competitors' strategies must be analyzed in order to avoid embarrassing interferences and similarity of the strategies. A brand should a priori chose exactly the field of operation and sponsorship, since dispersion across multiple sectors and events could confuse the consumers and dilute the brand image. Therefore a concentration on a field that is compatible with the brand's universe and roots is pivotal in order to develop a successful sponsorship strategy.[214]

4.5 People

People are an often-neglected part of a marketing strategy. Although this "P" is not included in the classic marketing-mix, it should be an integral part of luxury brand's marketing strategy. Basically it can be said that "people" refers to everyone who has connection with the brand, including customers, employees, and as mentioned above, celebrities or brand ambassadors. The customers of a luxury fashion brand as well as their motifs have already been discussed in detail in chapter 2.4. As well the roles of celebrities and brand ambassadors were shortly outlined Therefore this chapter will refer to the employees, especially the sales representatives and service staff. These are the people who have direct customer contact, represent the brand and therefore have a high level of responsibility. As already mentioned above, the sales assistants are those who need to "justify" the high price of a product or even better, seduce the customer to buy the product without even mentioning the price. In this process sales assistants play a key role: They have to explain the entire symbolic value, the high-precise work, the refinements and the details of the product to the customer. At best the customer gets the impression that, for

---

[213] Cp. Okonkwo, U. (2007), p. 156.

[214] Cp. Kapferer, J.N. / Bastien, V. (2009), p. 214 f.

the high quality he receives, the product is not even expensive.[215] To procure this ideal scenario sales assistants must meet certain requirements: They need to be highly professional, have expert knowledge about the brand, fit into the brand's universe according their looks and style, have good communication skills, maybe speak various languages and what is moreover important: they have to show empathy. According to literature one of the most customer complaints regarding luxury fashion stores and services is that the staff is cold, aloof, pretentious and arrogant.[216] This behavior is neither appropriate nor supporting for a luxury fashion brand. A good sales assistant reflects kindness, elegance, openness and support.

Since the luxury fashion consumers are often undecided what to buy for them personally or as a gift, the sales person needs to have knowledge of human nature. The trick is to guide the customers in a special direction without making them notice it, reassuring them in their choice and still let them feel like kings and queens.

A practical example to demonstrate how important sales employees are provides again Louis Vuitton. Here a store director has direct telephone access to the company's CEO and priority over all other departments. Another strategy applied by Louis Vuitton is that every newly employed manager has to coercive work in a Louis Vuitton store in order to gain a deeper understanding of the brand. This procedure should sharpen the understanding, how their later position can serve the sales network and therefore the customer.[217]

The importance of the sales-customer relationship indicates that a luxury brand must pay highest attention to the choice of their sales and service staff. Implications to maintain highest service standards could be that luxury fashion companies should provide its sales and service staff with ongoing training in communication, social as well as brand-related skills. Furthermore customer satisfaction studies could be designed to reveal strengths and weaknesses of the sales and service personnel and attain a better understanding of the customer's expectations.

4.6 Positioning

Although positioning occurs in this paper as the last point of the marketing strategy, it is actual the starting point for a luxury fashion company to create value from the brand and

---

[215] Cp. Kapferer, J.N. / Bastien, V. (2009), p. 192.

[216] Cp. Okonkwo, U. (2007), p. 164; Kapferer, J.N. / Bastien, V. (2009), p. 197. Amongst others.

[217] Cp. Kapferer, J.N. / Bastien, V. (2009), p. 235.

serves as cornerstone for the communication program.[218] A positioning strategy aims to attain a distinct, desired place of the brand in the consumer's mind and should generate emotions.[219] At first glance this appears to be easy in the case of fashion luxury brands, since the positioning "prestigious", "expensive", "well-crafted" and "high-end" are relatively apparent. But this is only the broad scope of positioning, which is more easily to implement. These features are common to all luxury brands. The real challenge for luxury fashion brands is the narrow scope of positioning. This part of the strategy really matters in order to be successful and competitive. Although the element of "luxury" might be overlapping, the brands still address different tastes and have different brand messages, what requires different positioning strategies. Basic requisitions for brand positioning are a clear, elaborated brand identity and a value proposition that should be communicated to the target group.[220] In the case of luxury goods the value proposition would be the intangible, ideal, dream value. The positioning of a brand should demonstrate advantages over competitors and ought to make it easy for the consumer to differentiate the brand from others. Positioning begins with associations created by images, words, products, prices and services that are communicated by the company. Through different mediums they find their way in the consumer's subconscious. However, it must be stated that only those elements of the brand identity should be communicated that really make a difference compared to competitor's brands. Only if the communicated elements are credible and distinctive, the consumer converts the associations into a guide and places the brand in a special location in his mind. Since the consumer has not only one, but many brands positioned in his mind, a clear brand understanding and perception is pivotal. Having obtained the right position, the brand plays an integral role in the consumer's selection process. In a purchase situation comparisons are drawn and the chance to be picked is higher, the better the consumer understood the benefits the brand generates for his life.[221] A definable, original and distinctive positioning of the brand becomes even more important if a company has a multi-brand portfolio or if a co-branding strategy is adopted. Both cases need clarification of the target-audience and the brand identities, in order to avoid cannibalization effects or confusion in the consumer's "mind-positioning-map".

Having attained a certain brand positioning within the customer's mind this does not mean that the brand has to remain there forever or it is not possible to alter the positioning.

---

[218] Cp. Aaker, D. (1966), p. 176.

[219] Cp. Okonkwo, U. (2007), p. 167.

[220] Cp. Aaker, D. / Joachimsthaler. E. (2000), p. 41.

[221] Cp. Okonkwo, U. (2007), p. 116 ff.

Changing circumstances in the business environment can fuel the need for a re-positioning strategy. In the case of luxury fashion brands this could become necessary due to the death or departure of a brand's master-designer or founder, changing consumer attitudes, e.g. the new conceptions of luxury, or modifications in the market place like globalization. However, a change in the positioning strategy does not necessarily imply a change of the brand identity or value proposition. A change in the positioning can be obtained by emphasizing another subset of the brand identity.[222] In the case of a re-positioning it is important that the consumer still recognizes the brand core but also the new elements of the positioning and that the fit between the old and new positioning is assured.[223]

However, a clear positioning is not only a benefit for the consumer, but also for the luxury fashion company itself. Especially on an internal decision level a look on the positioning map can be helpful, in order to evaluate product decisions like line extensions or diversification strategies.[224] Therefore the implication for a luxury brand is to develop a clear positioning for the consumers and for themselves. This can be achieved through detailed examination of one's own brand identity and the brand's distinguishing features, as well as benchmarking and a market analysis of the competitor's positioning. But besides the questions: Who are our target audience, what are the communication objects and what are our points of advantage, it is also crucial to make clear: What does the brand *not* stand for? If all these points are clarified the brand can work on a successful positioning strategy, establish competitive leverage and brand loyalty.

5 Outlook

Having examined different concepts of luxury, purchase motives and basic business implications for luxury fashion brands, the final question is: How will the future for luxury fashion brands look like? Although the luxury fashion market was and is not immune to crises and economic cycles, there will always be a demand for luxury fashion.[225] So what are the future developments and challenges this industry has to face and would imply future research?

---

[222] Cp. Aaker, D. (1966), p. 178.

[223] Cp. Meffert, H. / Burmann, C. / Kirchgeorg, M. (2008), p. 376.

[224] Cp. Okonkwo, U. (2007), p. 167.

[225] Cp. Appendix, Interview Peter-Paul Polte, p. 69; Interview Matthias Klein, p. 63.

The Internet will definitely play a more important role in future luxury fashion marketing strategies. As Brigitte Seebacher-Wolf stated it, luxury fashion brands cannot afford to neglect the Internet any longer. It is already a fundamental medium to search for information as well as to support brand communication and it will become an important distribution channel. Although luxury fashion brands are aware of these trends, they still hesitate to jump on the wave. [226] Many luxury fashion companies still consider the Internet more as a communication tool than as a transaction channel and are afraid that the Internet cannot convey a brand's heritage and long history. Furthermore they think that consumers need the opulent shopping experience in a physical store and want to display their ability to purchase a luxury product.[227] Considering a survey of the Luxury Institute among 1000 affluent customers that 98% purchase luxury goods on the Internet[228], the opponents of e-retail should rethink their attitudes again. Luxury brands must concentrate on maintaining their image through an aesthetic website, providing the consumers with latest news, collections, shopping possibilities and try to create the "luxury experience" through the Internet.

The next trend that must be paid attention to is customization. While some industry sectors already recognized the importance of customizing products it is only adopted to a little extent in the luxury fashion industry. Consumers nowadays are more demanding, since the wish for individualization is characterizing for our society. The wish for individualization can also be observed with fashion tastes and the desire to express personal creative potential. Consumer tastes are not predictable anymore. Especially luxury fashion consumers are innately demanding and desire exceptional, exclusive and total services and experiences from luxury brands. By offering the consumer the possibility to customize their product, individual needs and exquisite tastes can be satisfied. Furthermore, a satisfied customer is more likely to be a brand loyal customer. Apart from enhancing a deeper relationship with the brand, customization provides the brand with input of their customer's preferences and design expectations.[229] Looking back in history, luxury brands were born through made-to-fit products, which was later overtaken by mass-production. And although innovation should be one of the major facets of luxury fashion brands, many brands hesitate to go back to their roots. Opponents of customization strategies argue that by providing the customer with the tool to create their own products the brand would lose

---

[226] Cp. Appendix, Interview Brigitte Seebacher-Wolf, p. 79.

[227] Cp. Bruce, M. / Kratz, C. (2007) in Hines, T. / Bruce, M. (2007), p. 143.

[228] Cp. Birchall, J. (2007), Die Angst des Luxus vor dem Internet. In: FTD.

[229] Cp. Okonkwo, U. (2007), p. 247 ff.

its superior and exclusive image. However, the rules of the game have changed and a brand is more likely to lose its appeal, if thousands of costumers all over the world posses the identical, standardized product. As already explained in chapter 2.4, the need to distinguish themselves from others, to be special and unique is one major purchase motive of a luxury brand consumer that cannot be neglected. Marketers and designers need to understand that satisfying consumer's needs is pivotal to stay competitive in a changing business environment. Consequently, instead diminishing a brand's prestigious reputation, innovative approaches like customization and empathy for customer's needs enhance the brand image and value.

The third and last future trend that is shortly presented is the globalization of luxury fashion brands, due to the rise of new markets. Up to now China is the world's third largest consumer of luxury goods, according for 20% of the world consumption. Goldman Sachs predicts that China will be first in world consumption of luxury goods by 2015.[230] Another luxury market on the rise is India. According to the World Wealth Report 2008, India has the fastest growth of High Net Worth Individuals population, with 22.7%, a real GDP growth of 7.9%, a market capitalization growth of 118% plus the fastest growth of millionaires, which were 123.000 in 2007.[231] The third important future luxury market will be Russia. Although the country suffers from a lack of modern infrastructure, political turmoil and a declining population, the development of external relations is likely to improve the economic situation.[232] Especially the country's centers St. Petersburg and Moscow offer access to all international fashion luxury brands and it is estimated that over 100.000 inhabitants of Moscow fall in the range of those who can afford luxury goods.[233] Alone in Moscow shoppers spent up $2 to $4 billion a year on luxury goods and hence outrun New York City, where shopper spent $2 billion on high-end clothes and accessories.[234] These markets offer great expansion possibilities and will definitely be promising future markets.[235] However, the development and rise of future luxury fashion markets leads to the question of differences in cultural taste, preferences and concepts of luxury. How should a luxury fashion company proceed? Adopting the view of Dubois and

---

[230] Cp. N.N. (2005), China Becomes the World's Third Largest Consumer of Luxury Goods.

[231] Cp. World Wealth Report 2008, Capgemini & Merrill Lynch, p. 6.

[232] Cp. World Wealth Report 2008, Capgemini & Merrill Lynch, p. 7.

[233] Russia has 53 billionaires worth a total of $282 billion. In addition, the second-tier of riches includes 103,000 Russian millionaires who are collectively worth $670 billion. Cp. Weber, D. (2007), Not Down and Out in Moscow. In: The New York Times.

[234] Cp. Rozhon, T. (2004), Luxury Market Blooms Near Red Square. In: The New York Times.

[235] Cp. Appendix, Interview Peter-Paul Polte, p. 69.

Duquesne, a common set of shared values is central to any culture. Individuals of the same culture behave in a similar manner, have similar norms and reject or respect the same values. [236] As already explained above, luxury fashion products serve as a tool to express personal values and attitudes. In future luxury fashion brands are consequently confronted with the question how and if they should segment their markets. One approach would be to examine the values that a brand expresses and align them with the customer's cultural value system. A comparison between those gives hints to which extent the current marketing strategy regards cultural affinities.[237] On the other side it could be argued, that luxury brands have a certain essence that defines them and cannot be adjusted to cultural or regional preferences. In order to keep the prestigious status the consumers have to get along with the brand's values and not the other way round. It is a difficult, complex but also enthralling challenge luxury fashion brands have to face in future.

The future developments presented above and approaches to solve them will definitely provide material for further research and examination.

6 Conclusion

The goal of this paper was to develop marketing implications for luxury fashion brands. Therefore a holistic view on the landscape of fashion luxury products was provided, including theoretical constructs from several academic disciplines as well as practical points of view. The paper identified new trends of the conception of luxury, implying a shift from more tangible to intangible values. This goes along with new responsible, philanthropic consumer attitudes and hedonistic motives for the consumption of luxury products. Furthermore differences between consumer goods and luxury goods, regarding their benefits for the customer, were explained. Especially the current difficult market situation triggers executives, marketers but also researchers to re-think the situation of the luxury fashion industry. Some brands try to maintain high profits through brand extension, cutting costs where they think customers will not notice or even lowering prices.

Taking these findings into account the paper ought to develop practical implications and thought-provoking impulses. Summing up the major findings and implications it can be stated that luxury fashion brands need to focus on providing their customers with a holistic experience of luxury rather than "only" with a product. Experiences can be generated through several channels like services, clubs, events or sponsorships.

---

[236] Cp. Dubois, B. / Duquesne, P. (1993), p. 39.

[237] Cp. Dubois, B. / Duquesne, P. (1993), p. 43.

Fulfilling the consumer's needs is the competitive edge luxury fashion brands can obtain. This implicates to first understand the consumer's needs and then implement the new concepts of luxury into the brand strategy.

Especially in economic difficult times it is necessary for luxury brands to stand their ground. This means that instead to head for short-term profits and compromising the brand's value, luxury fashion brands should rather continue to demonstrate their strengths: Tradition, innovation, excellent quality, conviction and creativity. Although this means to temporarily maybe lose some customer's due to a constant high price level, the core of loyal customers will still remain and appreciate the brand's constant policy.

In addition it is important for fashion luxury brands to be open for new approaches and technologies. This comprises the integration of the Internet as an indispensable medium of our technique-affine society as well as tracking new trends like customization. Although a constant brand policy is an integral part of a luxury fashion brand, innovation and re-vitalization of the brand present no antagonism to that.

Fashion luxury brands must stay aware of current changes in society as well as in their business environment and compare these developments on a continuous level with their marketing strategy. If the right impulses are implemented in the brand's strategy, a fashion luxury brand has the best foundations to head towards new future challenges and success stories.

Appendix

Telefoninterview mit Matthias Klein, Investmentmanager und Repräsentant des Private Equity Fashion Fund One Fr2, 27.03.2009

Rebecca Glaser: Was macht für Sie eine Luxusmodemarke aus?

Matthias Klein: In erster Linie muss eine Luxusmarke eine Strahlkraft haben. Diese Strahlkraft sollte ein bestimmtes Image verkörpern, das selektiv ist. Dies bedeutet man bekommt diese Marke nicht überall, sie ist nur für einen bestimmten Käuferkreis erreichbar. Ist man also Besitz dieses Luxusproduktes, gehört man einer edleren Klasse an, man grenzt sich ab. Wir haben z.B. in unserem Portfolio eine französische Luxusmarke für Badehosen, Vilebrequin, für 120-360€ das Stück. Wenn man nackt ist dann hat man natürlich nichts, außer vielleicht seine Uhr und am Strand selbst die nicht. Dann ist man mit dieser Badehose also schon im Bereich Luxus. Der Träger weiß: Das ist etwas Besonderes. Beim Auto ist es z.B. im Vergleich zu Kleidung oder Uhren so, dass es einfach geparkt wird. Da gibt es nur den Schlüssel, wenn man im Cafe´ sitzt und dann weiß keiner, dass man einen Jaguar fährt. Daher muss man den Kern des Menschen treffen, was er sich gönnt und leistet und wie er das zeigen will. Für mich als Vertriebsprofi zählt aber ganz besonders ein exklusiver Vertrieb. Dann natürlich die Produktbeschaffenheit. Es muss eine Produktleistung, eine qualitative Leistung erkennbar sein. Bei einer Luxusmodemarke zahlt man natürlich mehr für das Image, aber dennoch muss die Produktqualität gut sein.

Rebecca Glaser: Sie haben gerade die Distribution erwähnt. Es zeichnet sich ein Trend ab, dass Luxusmodemarken zunehmend auf ihre eigenen Stores setzten. Halten Sie diese Konzentration auf die eigenen Stores für die geeignete Strategie, oder sind Sie der Meinung, dass es gewisse Lizenz- und Franchisekonzepte auch noch geben sollte?

Matthias Klein: Ich denke Luxusmarken können Franchisekonzepte haben, aber hier fängt natürlich eine sehr großes Steuerungsproblem an. Dies muss man auch bei Lizenzvergaben beachten. Wenn man Franchises oder Lizenzen vergibt muss man klare Vorgaben haben, man muss die Identität und das Image der Marke immer nach außen wahren.

Rebecca Glaser: Gab es Ihrer Meinung nach eine „Demokratisierung von Luxus", insbesondere auf die Textilbranche bezogen? Wenn ja, wo sehen Sie die Chancen und Risiken dieses Trends?

Matthias Klein: Das ist natürlich ein aktuelles Thema. Ich habe darüber einen Vortrag von Concetta Lanciaux gehört, die mit Bernard Arnault die LVMH Gruppe aufgebaut hat. Der Vortrag behandelte das Thema, wo die Marke bzw. das Produkt preislich positioniert ist. Wenn man dann die Preispositionierungen Unten, Mitte, Oben nimmt und einen Premium- mit einem Luxusmarkt vergleicht, dann sind die Grenzen von Premium zu Luxus immer die, die einen Einstiegspreis vermitteln können. Je nachdem welches Image und ideellen Nutzen eine Marke verkörpert, ist der Endverbraucher bereit bis zu einem bestimmten Punkt mitzugehen und verweigert sich dann. Das haben viele Luxusmarken jetzt auch erlebt. Das Setzen von Einstiegspreise erfordert hochsensible, vorsichtige Maßnahmen. Man muss auch psychologische Einstiegspreise beachten. Es geht eben nicht unendlich nach oben. Wenn man dann über den Preis eine Demokratisierung schafft ist das eine Sache, aber die andere Sache ist, dass Demokratisierung auch heißt „Wo vertreibe ich das Produkt?". Damit ist für mich der exklusive bzw. selektive Vertrieb gemeint, gekoppelt mit einem bestimmten Preis. Die Demokratisierung findet für mich aber mehr statt, indem eine Marke in Lizenzbereichen vorgeht und die absolute Demokratisierung bis hin zur Proletarisierung findet im Bereich von Lizenzen statt wie bei Duft. Das Thema Taschen wurde in den letzten Jahren auch immer wichtiger, es gab enorme Verkäufe bei Taschen. Eine Kundin kauft natürlich eher mal eine Tasche. Die nimmt man immer mit, die kann man zeigen und da ist man natürlich bereit mal mehr Geld auszugeben. Aber es sind natürlich auch interessante Einstiegspreislagen. Bei Duft ist es noch extremer, da ist die Verwenderin oder der Verwender jemand, der sich diese Marke sonst nicht leistet oder leisten kann. Man kauft sich dann eben Chanel. Damit hat der Käufer dann Bezug zu einer Luxusmarke. Für mich ist Demokratisierung also eine Abstimmung des sensiblen Preisgefüges und natürlich die Gefahr von Überdistribution. Die Preisaufbauten, Unten, Mitte, Oben und Luxus muss man in konkrete Preisbereiche definieren. Dies kann man am Beispiel Uhren sehen: Eine teure Uhr für 3000-4000€ kauft man sich mal, je nach dem wenn man kein Uhrenfan ist, alle 5-6 Jahre, wenn man sich mal etwas gönnen kann. Wenn jemand sich aber eine 15.000€ Uhr kauft, dieser Mensch kauft sich dann auch gern mal alle zwei Jahre eine neue, denn er hat dann nämlich das Geld. Da liegt dann aber die Grenze dazwischen. Wenn man z.B. die Rolex Daytona nimmt, gibt es diese in verschiedenen Ausführungen bis 20.000€, da kommt man schwer ran, dann ist es eine Mischung aus einer Premiumuhr, die aber einen besonderen Sammlerwert hat. Rolex ist für mich eine Demokratisierung von Luxus. Wenn man jetzt Armani nimmt stellt sich auch die Frage: Ist Armani jetzt Luxus oder ist Armani eine demokratisierte Premiummarke? Was denken Sie?

Rebecca Glaser: Ich denke Armani ist zur Zeit ein sehr schwieriger Fall. Auf der einen Seite kann man natürlich durch die Erweiterung der Marke um Armani eXchange und Armani Jeans sagen, dass eine Demokratisierung stattgefunden hat. Interessant ist jedoch auch, dass Armani nun zusätzlich eine Couture line entwickelt hat, um sich wieder höher zu positionieren. Des Weiteren hat sich die Marke durch Armani Casa auch in nicht-Kern Bereiche wie Möbel ausgedehnt.

Matthias Klein: Man muss sich immer fragen, ist das jetzt ein Lifestyle oder ein Luxus? Versace macht z.B. auch Porzellan. Es stellt sich die Frage, ob das etwas Besonderes ist, ist das erreichbar, kann ich das kaufen, wer sind die Verwender? Es ist bei Armani eben das Design, die Stilprägung aus einem Fashion Look, aus einer ikonografischen Markenbildung, die auch über das

Produkt kommt. Zusammenfassend gibt es meiner Meinung nach also eine Demokratisierung, diese hat aber was mit dem Preismix zu tun.

Rebecca Glaser: Die Luxusbranche galt lange Zeit als „krisensicher". Nun gibt es rückgehende Wachstumsprognosen für 2009. Was ist Ihre Zukunftsprognose für den Luxusmodemarkt, vor dem Hintergrund der Finanzkrise?

Matthias Klein: Dass auch diese Branche nicht krisensicher ist zeigten Ereignisse wie der 11. September, danach brach alles ein. Es gab eine SARS Entwicklung in China, dann konnten die Leute nicht mehr reisen. Die Asiaten sind nicht mehr nach z.B. London gekommen, der Luxusmarkt ist eingebrochen. Die reisenden, vermögenden Kunden konnten nicht mehr in die Metropolen fahren. Der Markt ist abhängig von Vielerlei, nicht nur von der Wirtschaft, sondern auch von Stimmungen, von Katastrophen, Trends. Die „neue Bescheidenheit" zum Beispiel. Es gab 1993, 1994, 1995 eine Zeit, da wurde Luxus verpönt. Eine Marke die in dieser Zeit entstanden ist, sind die Swatch-Uhren. Es war plötzlich „in", dass auch Manager eine Swatch für 70 Mark hatten. Es war einfach nicht mehr „in", eine Rolex zu tragen. So gesehen ist auch diese Branche nicht krisensicher. Wenn man aber Luxus macht, ist das immer eine langfristige Angelegenheit und Luxus wird immer überleben. Natürlich gilt das nicht für jede Marke. Jeder muss sich anstrengen und wenn man z. B. Louis Vuitton heute ist und sehr viel vertreten ist, müssen die auch ihre Marke auffrischen. Z.B. hat Louis Vuitton vor zwei Jahren auch neue Testimonials eingeführt, von Keith Richards bis hin zu Andre Agassi, also eine andere Kampagne gemacht und haben dabei vielleicht auch einmal eine andere Zielgruppe persönlich erreicht, durch ihr Marketing und ihre Werbung. Damit wären wir bei dem Thema Community Bildung. Und ein wesentlicher Treiber in den nächsten Jahren wird sein, dass man es schaffen muss, das gilt für alle Bereiche, ob low-, middle- oder high-price, sich Communities zu kreieren, also eine Fangemeinde zu bilden, die zu mir gehören, die zu meinem Angebot gehören wollen. Und die darf man nicht enttäuschen und muss immer wieder neue Dinge bringen, oder durch Verlässlichkeit, Tradition, Innovation und Neu-Interpretation überzeugen. Es gibt auch in diesen Zeiten im Luxusbereich Programme, die werden wachsen. Man wird Kunden finden, auch in einer Zeit die schwieriger ist, in der nicht jeder so leicht Geld ausgibt und sich auch der Einzelhandel dreimal überlegt, was er als Neues bringt. Aber bestimmte Besonderheiten sind auch in solchen Phasen immer wieder interessant. Wenn man z.B. Chanel nimmt, konnten diese mit einer wachsenden Luxuswelle mitschwimmen. Chanel hat dann mal vier, fünf Jahre Erfolg gehabt und jetzt werden sie wieder abgekühlt. Das ist ein Zyklus, gegen den man sich jetzt stellen muss, aber deswegen wird Chanel nicht vom Markt verschwinden. Chanel muss eben aufpassen, dass sie über das Produkt eine Neu-Interpretation erfahren und trotzdem ihrem Stil treu bleiben. Daher muss der Produktkern, die Aussage, die DNA von jemandem geführt werden. Und da ist es einfach sehr wichtig den Nerv zu treffen, den Markenwert, den Kern. Ich glaube, dass auf lange Sicht daher die Luxusbranche krisensicher ist, aber Trittbrettfahrer und normale Zyklen muss man auch hier akzeptieren. Der Luxusmodemarkt wird weitergehen, da gibt es überhaupt keine Diskussion. Die Menschen werden sich immer etwas Besonderes leisten können und wollen. Wenn das mal nicht so ist, dann ist das eine Phase. Die Kunst ist ja, dass die Wertschöpfung bei Luxusgütern höher sein kann, da sie sich einen Imagewert bezahlen lassen.

Rebecca Glaser: Das Aufeinandertreffen von Kreativen, z.b. Designern, und Managern wird oft als Problem der Modebranche thematisiert. Wo sehen Sie die Vor- und Nachteile bei eigen- und fremdgeführten Marken?

Matthias Klein: Wenn man ein Produkt entwickelt, eine Kollektion, eine Fashion Idee, dann verfolgt man ja auch allgemeine Trends. Natürlich haben wir heute ein Modezeitalter unter dem Begriff: Anything goes. Trotzdem gibt es natürlich einen sehr starken Mainstream Fashion Look. Es gibt bestimmte Trendmaterialen, es gibt bestimmte Trendthemen, Farbthemen... Wie setzt sich das Luxuslabel jetzt also ab? Ist es ein Luxuslabel alá Chanel, die auch mit Modefarben arbeiten, aber ihre klassischen Ideen behalten. Das ist die Wiedererkennbarkeit, die DNA die ein solches Produkt hat. Jetzt sagt aber der Manager auf der anderen Seite, dass man eine strategische Ausrichtung vornehmen muss, weil man die Marke dehnen muss. D.h. sie steht mehr für einen femininen Komplettlook. Aber man will z.b. auch eine Chanel casual Jeans Linie einführen, denn man muss die Marke weiterpushen. Dann will man damit natürlich auch andere Zielgruppen erreichen. Jetzt muss man den Designern das Konzept vorstellen, sie in ein Arbeitsgespräch einbinden und erklären "Das ist die Zielsetzung die ich verfolgen will, das ist die Strategie, wie wir das Ziel erreichen können." Wer führt dann das Ganze? Am Ende haben sie als Manager eine Idee, sind davon überzeugt, kommunizieren das nach Innen und nach Außen und dann kommt der Designer und arbeitet an dieser Idee. Dann dauert es auf einmal ein, zwei Jahre bis der Händler das übernimmt, bis der Endverbraucher das überhaupt wahrnimmt. Und dann stellt sich eben die Frage: Top oder Flop. Ein Bsp. wäre Burberry, die eine verschlafene Marke war aber durch einen Designer sehr strak wachgeküsst wurde aber wo auch das Marketing und das Produkt sehr gut ineinander gegriffen haben. Das Problem ist also, wer folgt an welcher Stelle wem und hat der Designer den Nerv des Endverbrauchers gepackt? Und wenn sich etwas nicht verkauft, dann liegt es eben an dem Produkt. Es gibt generell drei Gründe, warum sich ein Produkt nicht verkauft: Erstens die Produktqualität stimmt nicht, zweitens falsches Design, es geht am Geist des Endverbrauchers vorbei, oder drittens ein Vertriebsproblem, also Distribution. Und wenn man jetzt diese drei Punkte analysiert kann man am Punkt Vertrieb etwas machen, man kann auch am Produkt die Qualität verbessern, das geht beides systematisch. Aber das Design ist das Schwierigste und deswegen hängt eben sehr viel am Design. Karl Lagerfeld hat einmal gesagt: „Design ist keine demokratische Angelegenheit." Damit muss also einer die Richtung vorgeben und das ist immer dieser Konflikt, dass Designer sich unterordnen müssen und auch dem Konzept, dem Fashion Statement folgen müssen. Aber ohne gutes Design ist man als Manager eben nichts wert.

Es ist aber immer so, dass wenn Kollektionen entwickelt werden da immer mit System rangegangen wird, da gibt es einfache Schemen. D.h. wenn man jetzt eine Endverbraucherin nimmt, die Dior trägt und liebt, dann weiss man dieser Stil gefällt der Frau, dann hat man die DNA Dior erstmal. Dann schaut man sich den Kleiderschrank dieser Frau an, was für Marken trägt sie insgesamt, und teilt dies auf in ganz einfache Schemen. Basis-, Mittelmode und Fashion. Es ist eine Interpretationssache: Was ist Fashion für eine Frau, die gern Dior trägt? Ist es Dolce & Gabbana, ist es Roberto Cavalli? Also wie extrem geht sie und was sind die Basisprodukte? Und dann beschreibt man die Kundin und überträgt das auf seine Kollektion. Man macht ein Soziogram, eine präzise Beschreibung mit Alter, Einkommen, kauft diese Marken etc. und macht eine präzise Definition. Und genau diese Kundin will man erreichen, genau die *eine*, spezielle. Dass es dann noch Varianten gibt und sie vielleicht auch 10 Jahre älter sein kann, ist nur eine Variation. Wichtig ist, dass der Designer, der Manager und das Marketing eine Kundin im Kopf haben, die real zu erreichen ist. Dafür wird dann eine Kollektion entwickelt, die hat dann Basis-Mittel-, und Modeanteile, die hat dann auch City- und casual Anteile, Strickanteile und vielleicht noch Unterkollektionen. Aber man hat die *eine* vor Augen. Und diese Kundin wird auch jedes Jahr abgeglichen. Wie entwickelt sie sich weiter? Fährt sie jetzt ein anderes Auto, was gibt es neues drum herum? Dass man also diesen Weg mitgeht und trotzdem für diese Kundin auch eine verlässliche DNA dokumentiert. Dann ist es im Marketing auch so, dass die Manager und Designer gerne die die extremen Sachen, die Innovationen zeigen, dass man keine Langeweile versprüht. Und das muss zur Glaubwürdigkeit der Marke passen. Dazu kommt, dass sich viele Menschen die heute älter als 40 sind, noch 15 Jahre jünger im Kopf fühlen und im Marketing ist es wichtig, die Menschen natürlich auch mental zu erreichen. Des Weiteren ist das Verpacken wichtig, der Fit, dass etwas kleidet und gut aussieht, nicht nur auf dem Foto. Und deshalb ist Mode eine Ingenieursarbeit. Das wird oft von vielen vergessen, da stecken nicht nur tolle Stoffe dahinter, die werden auch ausgearbeitet, die werden passend gemacht. Die technischen Leute sind also ganz wichtig. Designer können tolle Ideen haben, aber wenn das nicht in einen Fit, in eine Silhouette passt, sind sie als Designer verloren. Das ist eben auch ein Aufeinandertreffen, dass es auch eine technische Leistung gibt. Davor warne ich immer: Schauen Sie nicht nur an der Oberfläche. Ein Beispiel wäre Bottega Veneta, das ist eine Handwerksarbeit, die haben die technischen Voraussetzungen und eine DNA. Die haben in den letzten zehn Jahren Stellenwert erreicht, durch ihre Einzigartigkeit, durch die Produktqualität, ohne dass sie einen Namen auf der Tasche nach außen tragen müssen. Man hat das Gefühl, man kauft ein hochwertiges, ein exklusives, ein mit Liebe erstelltes Produkt, technisch ausgearbeitet und ausgereift. Man ergattert ein Lieblingsteil, das man auch noch in zehn Jahren tragen kann. Dann stellt sich die Frage: Was macht der Kreative dabei? Es gibt natürlich Kreative, Designer. Aber die sind nicht so wichtig dabei. Es ist nicht so, dass man sagt: Man braucht nun Tom Ford um seine Marke wieder aufzuladen, sondern es ist einfach nur ein erstklassiges Produkt.

Abschließend ist in meinen Augen Markenführung generell immer Chefsache, man braucht einen Wächter der Marke.

Hiermit bestätige ich dieses Interview mir Frau Glaser am 27.03.2009 geführt zu haben:

(Matthias Klein)

20.04. 2009

Telefoninterview mit Peter-Paul Polte, Herausgeber Textilwirtschaft, 24.02.2009

Rebecca Glaser: Wie ist Ihre persönliche Definition von Luxus?

Peter-Paul Polte: Für mich ist Luxus alles, was über den normalen Bedarf hinaus geht, was man im Prinzip nicht braucht. Wobei die gegenwärtige Diskussion ja eher ist: Wie behaupten sich die Luxusmärkte in der Krise? Dies ist im Moment die größte und wichtigste Frage, mit der sich tausende von Menschen befassen.

Rebecca Glaser: Die Luxusbranche galt ja lange Zeit als „krisensicher". Dass dies nicht der Fall ist zeigen z.b. Entlassungen bei Chanel und rückgehende Wachstumsprognosen für 2009. Was ist Ihre persönliche Zukunftsprognose für den Luxusmodemarkt vor dem Hintergrund der Finanzkrise?

Peter-Paul Polte: Wenn man die Analysen der Aktienmärkte betrachtet, gab es vor kurzem schon einmal einen Tiefpunkt der Luxusindustrie, das war nach dem 11. September 2001. Danach sind die Aktien der Luxusanbieter massiv abgestürzt, wie ja alle Aktien. Da kam einiges zusammen. Der Tiefpunkt war im Frühjahr 2003. Ende März 2003 begann der Irak Krieg, die Aktienmärkte waren auf Ihrem Tiefpunkt, die Amerikaner sind nicht mehr nach Europa gereist. Das war die Zeit, in der die Geschäfte schon mal zusammengebrochen sind.

Rebecca Glaser: Dennoch ist die Branche in den letzten drei Jahren stetig gewachsen...

Peter-Paul Polte: Genau, nach dem Tiefpunkt ist in der Tat ein sehr starker Aufschwung gekommen. Inzwischen liegen auch die Zahlen für 2008 vor, auf die mit großer Spannung gewartet worden. Der erste Konzern der Im Januar veröffentlicht hat war Richemont, der meldet ein Minus von elf Prozent. Elf Prozent ist ein massiver Einbruch des Umsatzes mit entsprechenden Ertragseinbrüchen. Der zweite große Konzern der sehr früh gemeldet hat ist Luxottica, der Konzern der alle Designerbrillen herstellt, also auch die Produkte, die das Geld in die Kassen spülen. Auch er hat Negativzahlen gemeldet. Der nächste Konzern der dann veröffentlicht hat war Hermès, die sind gut durch das letzte Quartal gekommen, ungefähr mit plus 4 Prozent und haben das Jahr 2008 insgesamt sehr gut abgeschlossen. Das gleiche gilt für LVMH, auch die haben das Jahr 2008 gut abgeschlossen und haben auch nochmal 4% erreicht. Diese Konzerne hatten ein sehr gutes Weihnachtsgeschäft. In den nächsten Tagen werden weitere Veröffentlichungen folgen. Daraus kann man jetzt analysieren und es wird auch allgemein so gesagt: Die Konzerne, die im Grunde Familienkonzerne sind, sind bis jetzt ganz gut durchgekommen weil sie nicht unter dem Druck der Aktieninhaber stehen, Gewinn abwerfen zu müssen.

Rebecca Glaser: Wo sehen Sie In diesem Zusammenhang weitere Vor- und Nachteile von fremd- und eigengeführten Unternehmen?

Peter-Paul Polte: Die selbstgeführten Marken, also Familienunternehmen im Grunde, sind viel solider, haben eine relativ gute Kapitaldecke, stehen nicht unter dem Druck der Aktieninhaber und müssen keine Dividenden ausschütten. Sie haben relativ viel Geld zum Investieren und sind bankenunabhängig, was ihr großer Vorteil im Moment ist. Beim PPR Konzern z.B sieht es schlechter aus, der hat seine Zahlen letzte Woche veröffentlicht und hat ziemlich hohe Schulden zu bedienen, was sehr gefährlich ist. PPR selbst ist jedoch nicht schlecht aufgestellt, Gucci läuft sehr gut, Bottega Veneta läuft gut, im Gegensatz zu Yves Saint Laurent. Um die Frage nochmal zusammenzuführen, die familieneigenen Unternehmen werde die Krise deutlich besser bewältigen als die Aktiengesellschaften.

Rebecca Glaser: Um bei familien- oder besser gesagt designergeführten Unternehmen wie z.B. Dolce & Gabbana zu bleiben: Sehen sie es als Problem der Branche, wenn Manager und Designer zusammentreffen?

Peter-Paul Polte: Generell funktioniert das nicht. Bei Armani war es ja z.b. immer so, dass er einen Lebenspartner hatte, der alles gemanagt hat. Armani hat aber die Kurve gekriegt nach dem Tot von Galeotti und hat nun sehr gute Manger, die das Unternehmen führen. Dolce & Gabbana ist offensichtlich gut geführt, die Zahlen sind nicht negativ. Sie hatten jetzt Schwächephasen im Design, also im Kreativbereich, dadurch haben sie auch Umsatz verloren. Sie waren einfach nicht mehr so gut, da sie etwas zu arrogant geworden sind. Jetzt haben sie wahrscheinlich einen Dämpfer bekommen und werden nun etwas demütiger. Ansonsten ist Ferragamo noch eine finanziell sehr gut gepolsterte Familie. Fendi ist Familie, LVMH, Prada das sind alles solide geführte Unternehmen.

Rebecca Glaser: Was sagen sie zur derzeitigen Situation von Escada?

Peter-Paul Polte: Escada ist im Moment eine Katastrophe, der Konzern ist ja eine Aktiengesellschaft und die Aktie ist total runter, sie ist ein Penny-Stock geworden. Sälzer ist ein sehr guter Mann und müsste es eigentlich schaffen und hat natürlich Pech, weil die großen, wichtigen Märkte Russland und Amerika eingebrochen sind, was er vor einem Jahr natürlich nicht erwartet hat, als er den Job angenommen hat. Die Herz Familie hat ja Geld, also ist wahrscheinlich erstmal im Stande das zu finanzieren. Irgendwann mal muss er natürlich die Wende hinbekommen, ob er das schafft bin ich im Moment auch nicht im Stande zu sagen.

Rebecca Glaser: Sie haben gerade die großen Märkte angesprochen, sehen sie es als zukunftsweisend für die Luxusmodeunternehmen, sich auf die neuen Märkte wie Russland, China, vielleicht auch bald Indien zu konzentrieren?

Peter-Paul Polte: Eine Konzentration auf diese Märkte auf gar keinen Fall. Die Hauptumsätze werden ja immer noch in Europa und Amerika gemacht, also in den reichen Industrieländern. Das sind auch die luxusaffinen Märkte und hier sind auch die meisten Geschäfte. Indien ist immer noch ein sehr armes Land, China ist ein Land das gerade erwacht, natürlich sind das die Zukunftsmärkte. Russland ist ein kleines Land, zwar flächenmäßig riesig, aber menschenmäßig klein. Russland hat nicht mehr als 150 Mio. Menschen, die potenzielle Kundschaft ist also relativ gering. Wenn Sie dann unsere Kernländern in Europa als Vergleich nehmen, wir sind 320 Mio. reiche Westeuropäer mit unendlich viel Vermögen, also hier steckt das Geld. Ich habe einen Vortrag von einem Russlandexperten gehört der sagte, wenn man mal den Großraum Moskau nimmt, wo ja 10 oder 12 Mio. Menschen leben, die haben ein paar Autobahnen die reichen 50 km aus Moskau raus, dann hören sie auf. D.h. man kauft sich einen Porsche und nach 50 km hört die Autobahn auf. Dann ist der Porsche auch sinnlos. Und hier kann man durch ganz Europa mit dem Porsche jagen. Von Indien brauchen wir in diesem Zusammenhang gar nicht zu reden. Jedoch, in den nächsten 30-40 Jahren werden das bestimmt ganz tolle Märkte, Gott sei Dank, das ist ja auch unsere Hoffnung. So eine Krise wird auch irgendwann zu Ende sein und die Menschen wollen immer das haben, was die reichen Leute auch haben. Z.B. 1945 hat alle Welt nach Amerika geschaut. So muss man sich das jetzt auch vorstellen. Osteuropa z.B. wird auch noch sehr stark kommen, das sind unsere Zukunftsmärkte, natürlich.

Rebecca Glaser: Abschließend würde mich noch interessieren, wie denn für Sie eine gelungene Marketingstrategie für eine Luxusmodemarke aussieht?

Peter-Paul Polte: Da gibt es ja gewisse Grundregeln. Eine der wichtigsten Grundregeln ist Verknappung. Bei Hermès z.B. ist das Prinzip der Verknappung ist ganz, ganz massiv. Die Verknappung, sagen wir mal die Mystifizierung ist grundlegend. Deshalb haben ja alle großen Luxusmarken eigene Läden, sie wollen sich selbst inszenieren, sie investieren viel Geld in die Inszenierung.

Rebecca Glaser: Sehen Sie diese Inszenierung durch line-extensions gefährdet wie z.B. bei Armani, der jetzt mit Armani Casa auch Möbel designt?

Peter-Paul Polte: In gewisser Weise ja. Ich würde das auch nicht so machen. Von Armani möchte ich persönlich beispielsweise auch keine Möbel haben, das finde ich ein bisschen unsinnig. Es versuchen ja aber im Grunde viele Konzerne heute. Hermès macht dies zum Teil auch, nur viel zurückhaltender, also Wohnaccessoires ist sicherlich ein Thema was ich ganz gut finde. Was sich aus der Kernmarke ergibt ist sicherlich erfolgreich, sprich Bekleidung, Schuhe, Lederwaren, Duft, Kinderkleidung, Strümpfe, Accessoires, Brillen. Das ist alles noch sehr verbunden mit der Kernmarke. Bei Möbeln sehe ich das kritisch, ich glaube auch nicht, dass die Welt auf Möbel von Armani wartet, dazu gibt es sicherlich genügend andere. Ich denke, das ist irgendeine fixe Idee von ihm. Was ich nicht schlecht finde ist die Ausdehnung in Luxushotels, was auch immer mehr Konzerne machen. Also eine bestimmte Welt umsetzen in ein Luxushotelkonzept, das machen Ferragamo, Bulgari, Versace, Armani und es scheint um sich zu greifen.

Man muss natürlich schon aufpassen, wie weit man sich ausbreitet. Louis Vuitton hat ja bereits 420 Läden weltweit, was sehr viel ist, Hermès hat vielleicht 300. Dann gibt es ja auch den Fall Pierre Cardin, der zeitweilig 800 Lizenzen vergeben hat, das ist gar nicht mehr zu kontrollieren. Es gibt dann Krawattenhersteller in Korea, in China, in Deutschland, in Amerika, überall... Das war auch die Gefahr in diesem Fall und Pierre Cardin hat die Lizenzen dann auch heruntergefahren. Mit Lizenzvergaben sind die Konzerne generell alle vorsichtig. Man hat das in der Vergangenheit gemacht, Dior waren die ersten nach dem Krieg, und heute ist die Tendenz eher, die Lizenzen zurückzunehmen, weil man die Produkte selbst kontrollieren will. Strenesse z.b. merkte auch, dass man bei Lizenzvergaben aufpassen muss. Plötzlich bringt jemand Schuhe unter dem Namen Strenesse, die ganz schlecht sind, das hat dann negative Rückwirkungen auf die Kernmarke. Dann ist natürlich das Preis Thema. Soll man im Zuge der Krise mit den Preisen runtergehen? „Nein, bloß nicht!", warnen alle davor! Man darf nicht die Kompetenz verwässern. Der Preis ist ein ganz gefährliches Thema, auch bei Zweitmarken.

Hiermit bestätige ich dieses Interview mir Frau Glaser am 24.02.2009 geführt zu haben:

Peter Paul Polte

(Peter-Paul Polte)

Telefoninterview mit Dipl.-Kfm. Axel Schübeler, ProSpector®, Qualitative Marketingberatung

Rebecca Glaser: Was genau haben Sie für Hugo Boss gemacht?

Axel Schübeler: Was wir gemacht haben war eine kleine Studie für die Marke HUGO, wo es darum ging ins Blaue hinein zu schauen: Wer sind die Menschen, die HUGO kaufen, sowohl bei Men´s als auch bei Woman´s Wear, weil man letztlich im Hause Boss kein konkretes Bild davon hatte, wer die Ware später wirklich aus dem Regal nimmt. Wir sind so vorgegangen, dass wir uns verschiedene Stores ausgesucht haben, das war z.b. der HUGO Mega Store in Berlin, der nur die Marke HUGO als Flagshipstore sozusagen führt, es war ein Szeneladen in München dabei, „Stierblut", dann hatten wir ein Kaufhaus in Freiburg dabei, das die Marke HUGO auf einer eher spießigen Ebene angeboten hat und wir hatten den P&C in Frankfurt dabei. Also die ganzeDistribution einmal durch. Und da sind wir einfach in die Läden gegangen, da wir ja gar nicht wussten: Wen rekrutieren wir, wen suchen wir eigentlich? Man hätte die gar nicht auf der Straße finden können und darum haben wir uns einfach mit unseren Interviewern vor Ort Menschen angeschaut, also wirklich im Sinne eines stillen Beobachters. Das heißt: Wer kommt in den Laden, wer kauft was, wer kauft wieviel? Dann haben wir diese Personen angesprochen, ob sie Zeit und Lust hätten für ein kurzes Gespräch, das wir in dem Shop dann geführt haben. Da ging es letztlich um ein sehr offenes Gespräch. Wir sind ja ein qualitativ-psychologisches arbeitendes Institut, das heißt wir haben keinen Fragebogen entwickelt, sondern wirklich ein offenes, leitfadengestütztes Gespräch. Da haben wir die Person dann einfach gefragt, wie sie zur Marke HUGO gekommen sind, wie sie die Marke erleben, was die Abgrenzung zu anderen Marken ist, was die Position der Marke HUGO innerhalb der Range von Boss ist. Und auch ein paar Fragen zu deren Leben, was für Hobbies sie haben, wie viel Geld sie für Kleidung ausgeben, wo sie gerne shoppen, welche Medien sie nutzen usw. Einfach um ein Gefühl zu bekommen, wer ist das, der tatsächlich die Marke HUGO kauft.

Rebecca Glaser: Wann genau hat die Studie stattgefunden? Ich frage deswegen, weil ich es sehr interessant finde, dass HUGO, was ja im Grunde genommen eine etablierte Modemarke ist, bis zu diesem Zeitpunkt noch nichts über ihre Zielgruppe wussten.

Axel Schübeler: Das ganze hat vor circa einem Jahr stattgefunden. Wir haben das im Januar/Februar durchgeführt und im März präsentiert. Es ist nicht ungewöhnlich für Modemarken, dass sie ziemlich viel schauen: Was sind die Trends, was sind die Hypes, was sind die no-gos, was sind die Szene-locations etc., aber eigentlich nicht wirklich schauen, wer sind die Menschen, mit denen ich zu tun habe? Und das war für das Haus Boss auch erstmalig, dass sie sowas gemacht haben, das haben sie vorher noch nie gemacht.

Rebecca Glaser: Denken Sie also, dass bei der Marketingstrategie von Luxusmodemarken der Kunde vernachlässigt wird?

Axel Schübeler: Also ich kann jetzt nicht für die anderen Marken sprechen, sonder nur dafür, was ich als Konsument erlebe, sprich die Ansprache des Verbrauchers über Massenmedien oder die Ansprache im Shop, aber prinzipiell würde ich sagen „ja". Ich würde da aber auch differenzieren. Wenn man bei dem Wort Luxusmodemarke das Wort Mode in den Mittelpunkt rückt, demokratisiert man natürlich auch den Luxus sehr. Mode ist etwas vergängliches, Mode ist etwas, was die breite Masse anspricht, sonst wird es gar nicht Mode. Marken die sehr demokratisiert sind, wie Boss das ja auch ist, stehen viel mehr in der Pflicht, sich den Kunden genauer anzuschauen, während echte Luxusmarken, die also wirklich High-end Luxus, sind, die müssen das nicht. Die leben ja teilweise auch davon, dass sie eine gewisse Arroganz an den Tag legen und sagen: Wir sind wer wir sind und haben es gar nicht nötig uns nach unseren Käufern zu richten, der Käufer soll doch froh sein, dass er uns überhaupt kaufen kann. Ich sage mal eine Dose Beluga Kaviar, ob die nun inconvenient zu öffnen ist oder ein schlecht zu lesendes Rückenetikett hat, der ist das relativ egal. Auch der CO_2 footprint eines Kobe-Rindsteaks, oder ob eine Uhr von Lange und Söhne bequem von Winter- auf Sommerzeit umzustellen ist, darum geht es nicht. Da geht's um Perfektion und Tradition und diese zwei Dinge sind stark miteinander verknüpft. Und solche Marken, also die ich als echte Luxusmarkensehe, das ist natürlich auch eine Definitionssache, die schauen in der Regel nicht nach ihrem Verbraucher, die müssen auch nicht nach ihrem Verbraucher schauen,sondern die machen einfach nur ihr Ding. Die haben auch keine Einstiegsmarken, die haben keine Outlet-Stores und allein daran kann man schon eine ganze Menge ablesen. Aber gängige Modemarken wie Boss, Armani, Joop, die sind viel mehr verpflichtet sich den Kunden genauer anzuschauen.

Rebecca Glaser: Ich denke man kann das generell für den Bereich Mode sagen. Ich behaupte, dass Marken wie Hermès, Louis Vuitton oder Bottega Veneta, die meiner Meinung nach auch *echte* Luxusmarken sind, trotzdem auf den Kunden schauen müssen, da in diesem Markt eine unglaubliche Konkurrenz vorhanden ist.

Axel Schübeler: Klar, genau das ist die Bandbreite. Das fängt unten an bei C&A und hört oben bei den von Ihnen genannten Marken auf. Das ist so ein Kontinuum, und je weiter man oben ist, desto mehr kann man seinen Charakter setzen und je weiter unten man ist in diesem Kontinuum, desto mehr muss man gucken, wie kann ich den überzeugen, der mich kaufen soll. So würde ich das wahrnehmen.

Rebecca Glaser: Um wieder auf die Studie zu kommen: Was haben sie denn rausgefunden über die HUGO Kunden. Was sind die Kaufmotive, was macht den Kunden aus?

Axel Schübeler: Also die Kaufmotive haben wir nicht untersucht, wir haben hauptsächlich geschaut: Wer ist das und was suchen die in der Marke. Es war ja eine Ihrer Fragen im Vorfeld, ob der Trend vom Prestigekauf weg, hin zum Kauf aus hedonistischen Motiven geht. Wir haben jeweils 5 verschiedene Typologien, also typische Verwender sowohl bei Männlein als auch bei

Weiblein gefunden. Wobei relativ viele, ich glaube es waren drei oder vier Typen, waren äquivalent als weibliche und männliche Ausprägung. Und es gab z.B. eine ältere Dame und einen älteren Herrn, die aber aus ganz unterschiedlichen Beweggründen eine junge Marke wie HUGO gekauft haben. Von daher ist es schwer über einen Kamm zu scheren, was die Gründe waren, warum die Leute die Marke gekauft haben. Die hedonistische Perspektive würde ich sagen bedingt, da Deutsche ja sowieso eher die sind, die das Etikett gerne Innen tragen, wohingegen ein Russe oder ein Amerikaner das Etikett doch sehr gerne Außen trägt und damit entsprechend protzt. Und das ist bei Deutschen ja sowieso nicht so, von daher ist dieses hedonistische für mich prinzipiell stärker ausgeprägt als in anderen Nationen. Aber ich denke, dass die soziale Komponente, der Vergleich, die Show, das Prestige, wie auch immer sie das nennen wollen, trotzdem wichtig ist. Ich glaube auch: Im Moment kommt es zu einer ganz klaren Verschiebung im Umgang mit Prestige, aufgrund der wirtschaftlichen Situation weltweit. Einerseits in einem zeitlichen Ablauf, dass eine Demokratisierung des Luxus stattfand, man konnte eben Champagner auch bei Aldi kaufen, wodurch sich Definitionen einfach verschoben haben. Ich glaube nicht, dass dadurch Champagner auf einmal mehr oder weniger Prestige hatte. Aber Champagner alleine war es eben nicht mehr, mit dem man bestimmte Symbolik ausdrücken konnte. Es war halt dann nur noch der Piper-Heidsieck und Champagner selbst sagte nichts mehr aus, denn es konnte eben von...bis gehen. Das hat sich, glaube ich, auch bei den Modelabels gezeigt, dass eben viele, die nicht so am oberen Ende der Luxusrange angesiedelt sind, wie Boss, Armani, Joop, dass die eben auch etwas erodiert sind und nicht mehr zu den Prestigemarken gehören, aber auch noch nicht diesen Charakter haben, dass sie so etwas hedonistisches selbstzufriedenes haben. Der Umgang mit Luxus wird im Moment neu sortiert und die Karten sind da vielleicht noch nicht alle verteilt, aber für die sichtbaren Prestigemarken würde ich sagen sind die Karten nicht so gut für die nächste Runde wie für die, die den hedonistischen, privaten Luxus bieten. Die haben bessere Chancen in Zukunft.

Rebecca Glaser: Was mich noch interessieren würde sind die fünf Käufertypologien. Können Sie diese kurz charakterisieren? Was war das Gesamtergebnis der Studie?

Abel Schübeler: Also das Ergebnis war, dass Boss über einige Typen erstaunt war, dass sie die ansprechen, bei einigen Typen hocherfreut war, dass diese dabei waren und bei einigen Typen wirklich schon fast gesagt hat, die wollen wir gar nicht haben. Es war also schon ein sehr hoher Überraschungswert dabei. Wir hatten bei den Männern einen Typ dabei der hieß „Pink Panther", der war eher aus der Homosexuellenszene, aus der Kreativszene, Leute die wirklich sehr viel Wert auf ihr Outfit gelegt haben und auch einen sehr hohen Geldbetrag regelmäßig dafür ausgegeben haben und mit sehr schrägen Klamottenkombinationen aufgewartet haben, also echte Szenegänger die im Künstlerischen zu Hause waren. Die haben auch häufig Boss Orange gekauft, die etwas schräge, trashige Linie und mit HUGO einfach nur ihr Set mit den Essentials ergänzt, also z.B. das weiße Hemd, das man immer dazu tragen kann, das war dann eben ein HUGO Shirt. Für die war HUGO eben überhaupt keine hippe Marke, sondern die, die die Basics geliefert hat. Dann gab es einen Typ den haben wir den „Dream Boy" genannt, das war wirklich der, auf den

HUGO sich von ihrer Marketingstrategie fokussiert haben, ein Sunny-boy, total smarter Typ, ungekünstelt, auch auf der Sonnenseite des Lebens stehend was seine Karriere und sein Einkommen anbelangt, aber auch einer der mal an der Ecke an der Pommesbude stehen kann und gerne ein Schwätzchen hält. Bei den femininen Typen hatten wir vier unterschiedliche.

Wir konnten diese dann auch noch soziodemografisch beschreiben, haben sie dann bebildert mit Fotos, die wir in den Shops gemacht haben, so dass Bossein Gefühl dafür bekommen konnte, wer das denn eigentlich ist. Boss war mit diesen Typen sehr zufrieden und hat das dann auf einen Fragebogen runtergebrochen, welchen sie dann quantifizierend in mehreren Ländern eingesetzt haben.

Hiermit bestätige ich dieses Interview mir Frau Glaser am 31.03.2009 geführt zu haben:

(Axel Schübeler)

Telefoninterview mit Brigitte Seebacher-Wolf, Head of Strenesse Public Relations International, 11.03.2009

Rebecca Glaser: Auf der Strenesse Homepage wird von „spürbarem" Luxus gesprochen. Wie ist die genaue Definition von Luxus bei Strenesse?

Seebacher-Wolf: Im Prinzip heißt Luxus für uns, dass die Marke in jeder Hinsicht qualitativ hochwertig ist. Gabriele Strehle legt sehr viel Wert auf die Materialien, das Design, den Schnitt und die Verarbeitung. Der Kern ist, die Liebe zum Detail in jeder Hinsicht und daraus resultiert im Endeffekt auch der Luxus, dass es wirklich Materialen sind durch die man spürt, dass man sich etwas gönnt aber, dass das ganze auch eine gewisse Langlebigkeit hat. Das ist auch der Unterschied von Strenesse zu anderen Luxusmarken, dadurch dass soviel Wert auf Qualität gelegt wird, kann man es auch länger tragen. Es ist also nicht nur ein Fashion item, das man eine Saison trägt, und dann kann man es entweder nicht mehr anziehen oder es ist einfach kaputt gegangen, sondern es ist langlebig und zeitlos.

Rebecca Glaser: Meine zweite Frage bezieht sich auf die Demokratisierung von Luxus in der Textilbranche. In der aktuellen Diskussion wird oft gesagt, dass sich im Prinzip jeder ein Stück Luxus leisten kann. Gibt es diese Demokratisierung wirklich und wenn ja, wo sind die Chancen bzw. Risiken dieses Trends?

Seebacher-Wolf: Das ist eine ziemlich schwierige Frage. Es kommt im Prinzip darauf an, wie man Luxus definiert. Klar ist es so, dass mehr sich heutzutage Luxus leisten können, weil jeder Luxus für sich anders definiert. Für den einen ist Luxus z.B. sich ein Kleid von Gabriele Strehle zu kaufen, weil man es für einen bestimmten Anlass braucht, weil man einen Business Termin hat oder auf eine Abendveranstaltung geht. Für den anderen kann Luxus sein, dass man sich Zeit nimmt am Wochenende etwas mit meiner Familie zu unternehmen, oder sich die Zeit nimmt, sich am Nachmittag in den Garten zu sitzen und einen Kaffee zu trinken. Aus diesem Aspekt betrachtet kann sich Luxus heutzutage schon jeder leisten.

Rebecca Glaser: Meine dritte Frage bezieht sich auf die aktuelle Finanzkrise. Wie ist Ihre Zukunftsprognose für den Luxusmodemarkt und vor allem, wie geht Strenesse mit dieser Krise um?

Seebacher-Wolf: Im Prinzip ist es so, dass die Krise natürlich da ist. Man liest viel darüber, man sieht Insolvenzen am Automarkt, eine so traditionelle Marke wie Schiesser ist insolvent, also die Krise greift um sich. Wie die Entwicklung weiter gehen wird kann man meiner Meinung nach noch nicht absehen. Es ist ein bisschen wie Glaskugel lesen. Jeder rechnet damit, aber im Prinzip kann man es nicht voraussagen und vielleicht wird es ja gar nicht so schlimm, wie alle denken. Es wird sicherlich ein wahnsinnig spannendes Jahr werden und es wird sicherlich viel passieren. Die Einstellung von Gabriele Strehle ist, und das sieht man auch in der aktuellen Kollektion, dass man die Krise auch durchaus positiv sehen kann. Es gibt ja das Zitat von Max Frisch der sagt: "Ich finde dass die Krise ein ungemein produktiver Zustand ist, man muss ihr nur den Beigeschmack der Katastrophe nehmen." Aus der Krise heraus kann also auch durchaus etwas Positives entstehen.

Rebecca Glaser: Worauf muss Ihrer Meinung nach bei einer gelungenen Marketingstrategie für Luxusmodemarken Rücksicht genommen werden? Was ist das Besondere an der Strenesse Marketingstrategie?

Seebacher-Wolf: Im Prinzip muss bei einer gelungenen Marketingstrategie darauf geachtet werden, dass mit allen Aktivitäten die man macht die Markenwerte transportiert werden. Und es ist auch gerade im Luxusbereich wichtig, dass man seiner Marke treu bleibt. Gerade im Luxusmodemarkenbereich kann man es sich nicht leisten, sich da zu verzetteln. Man muss auch ganz genau schauen, passt das was ich gerade mache auch zu meiner Zielgruppe? Es macht keinen Sinn, wenn ich eine Luxusmarke wie Strenesse bin, meine Zielgruppe ist 35+ und ich setzte den Fokus meiner Kampagne auf YouTube oder MyVideo.
Wir können auch solche Elemente Below the line einssetzen, da es zu unserer zweiten Linie Strenesse Blue ganz gut passt. Generell muss man sich ganz genau überlegen was man macht und dass es auch zur Marke passt. Als Luxusmarke kann man einfach nicht alles machen.

Rebecca Glaser: Es hat sich am Anfang ja auch die Frage gestellt, wie das Internet im Luxusmodemarkensegment überhaupt genutzt werden soll. Das hat sich inzwischen schon geändert. Inzwischen kann man auf der Homepages vieler Luxusmarken auch schon die Produkte bestellen. Fördert dies Ihrer Meinung nach, dass die Marke als Luxusmodemarke wahrgenommen wird, oder wird das Image geschädigt?

Seebacher-Wolf: Ich sehe das nicht so. Ich bin der Meinung, dass das Medium Internet wahnsinnig wichtig ist, auch für Luxusmarken, weil es einfach heutzutage ohne das Internet nicht mehr geht, man kommt nicht daran vorbei. Gerade im Luxusmarkensektor hat man das Medium Internet sehr spät für sich entdeckt. Auch wenn man generell schaut passiert auf den Markenseiten sehr wenig. Auch wir haben letztes Jahr erst eine neue Seite gelauncht und die ist jetzt langsam im Aufbau. Luxusmarken setzen schon immer noch sehr viel auf die klassische Kommunikation, auf Printwerbung und ich habe das Gefühl man hat das Medium noch nicht hundertprozentig für sich entdeckt. Wenn man sich jetzt aber mal die Chanel Seite anschaut, ist diese immer up-to-date. Die haben immer etwas Neues, die machen z.B. sehr viel mit dem Medium Internet. Es ist einfach von Unternehmen zu Unternehmen unterschiedlich. Ich glaube, das Bewusstsein, dass das Internet ein wahnsinnig wichtiges Medium ist um Botschaften an den Mann zu bringen ist schon da. Es ist nur von Unternehmen zu Unternehmen, und auch innerhalb der Abteilungen sowie bei den Unternehmern selber unterschiedlich, wie internetaffin diese sind. Für uns, für Strenesse, ist das Medium Internet ein sehr wichtiges. Ich habe in unserer Marketingstrategie das Internet sehr stark drinnen. Wir wollen einen großen Onlineshop aufbauen, der im September online gehen wird, den wir auch online bewerben werden, weil gerade die Möglichkeit im Internet zu shoppen ein zusätzlicher Vertriebskanal ist, der nicht unterschätzt werden darf. Es wird wahnsinnig viel Umsatz im Internet gemacht, gerade auch im Luxusmarkenbereich. Auch generell bin ich der Meinung, dass man eine Marke viel mehr beleben kann, wenn sich auf der Internetseite was tut. Egal ob das nun ein Bewerber ist oder ein Student der seine Diplomarbeit schreibt und Informationen sucht, oder ein Journalist, der sich über etwas informieren will. Meistens ist der erste Weg heutzutage auf die Website und man schaut was ist da drauf, was kann ich hier über die Marke erfahren.

Rebecca Glaser: Besonders interessant finde ich bei Strenesse, dass sowohl die Designer als auch die Manager in der Familie sitzen. Wie werden denn wichtige Entscheidungen im Unternehmen getroffen, werden zusätzlich externe Experten hinzugezogen?

Seebacher-Wolf: Im Prinzip ist es so, dass wir bei Strenesse in der glücklichen Lage sind, Experten aus allen Bereichen zu haben. Auf der einen Seite ist ein sehr starker Pol natürlich die Familie, bestehend aus Gerd Strehle, der auch der Kopf des Unternehmens ist und auf der wirtschaftlichen Seite agiert und alles was PR und Marketing angeht regelt. Dann gibt es Gabriele Strehle, die als quasi „Herz" der Marke und Chefdesignerin verantwortlich für die ganzen Kollektionen ist und den Design-Pol sehr stark darstellt. Dann Viktoria Strehle, die ja eigentlich eher eher aus der Sales Richtung kommt und seit Februar 2008 das Kreativ Team von Strenesse Blue leitet. Sie ist darüber hinaus verantwortlich für die Accessories, für unsere eigenen Shops, das heißt sie ist sowohl als auch tätig. Sie arbeitet mit Gabriele Strehle sehr eng an den Kollektionen, aber sie ist auch sehr vertriebsorientiert, da sie auch für die Umsätze der Shops verantwortlich ist und weil sie auch aus dem Verkauf kommt. Das heißt innerhalb der Familie gibt es eigentlich nicht nur zwei Pole, sondern es gibt eigentlich drei. Zusätzlich gibt's natürlich in allen Bereichen Abteilungsleiter. Das ist dann schon ein Pool aus mehreren Leuten die die Entscheidungen dann treffen, das macht nicht die Familie im kleinen Kämmerchen.

Rebecca Glaser: Mich hätte noch interessiert, wie Sie die Situation im Allgemein in der Branche einschätzen. Wenn Kreative und Manager aufeinandertreffen sind das oftmals sehr entgegengesetzte Weltbilder.

Seebacher-Wolf: Das kommt vor, aber das ist nichts Negatives. Klar, der Designer hat ganz genaue Vorstellungen wie das Produkt ausschauen soll, wie er das an den Mann bringen will, was das Produkt können soll und wie das Produkt kommuniziert werden soll. Der Manager hat da natürlich etwas andere Vorgaben, er muss das Produkt ja auch verkaufen und in eine Kampagne setzen. Das heißt klar gibt es dann auch oft Kompromisse, dass man sagt: Ja, das Teil ist super, aber es verkauft sich in gelb nicht, wir brauchen das unbedingt in rot, als Beispiel. Dann man muss eben argumentieren. Gerade unsere Kollektionen sind ja sehr von Gabriele Strehles Stil geprägt und sie hat natürlich bei der Kollektion das letzte Wort. Aber es ist nicht so bei uns, dass die Kreativen auf Wolke sieben schweben und nicht mitkriegen, was draußen im Handel passiert. Es gibt ja auch Leute wie z.b. Viktoria die im Markt draußen sind, die genau das Wissen vom Markt reinbringen. Also ich glaube auch, diese strikte Trennung zwischen dem Kreativen und dem Management gibt es heutzutage gar nicht mehr. Das kann sich ein Unternehmen auch gar nicht leisten. Das war früher bestimmt viel stärker, aber heute sind die Designer schon bereit auch Kompromisse einzugehen. Aber klar, es gibt dieses Aufeinanderprallen nach wie vor und es gibt auch bei uns viele Diskussionen. Der Verkauf kommt dann mit Ideen und hätte das gern und die Kreation sagt: Auf keinen Fall machen wir das. Aber letztendlich entsteht dann ein fruchtbares Gespräch und am Schluss gibts dann eine Lösung, die dann so oder so aussieht. Also es ist nicht so, dass dann beide Parteien beleidigt sind und nicht mehr miteinander sprechen. Irgendeine Lösung gibt immer.

Rebecca Glaser: Meine letzte Frage wäre, ob sich an der Marketingstrategie etwas geändert hat, als Strenesse zur AG wurde?

Seebacher-Wolf: Dazu bin ich zu kurze Zeit im Unternehmen. Aber dass es eine AG wurde hat sich auf die Marketingstrategie nicht ausgewirkt, soweit ich weiß. Das ist eine reine Sache auf dem Papier, denn das Unternehmen ist zwar eine AG, ist aber immer noch im Familienbesitz. An der Marketingstrategie hat sich eher etwas geändert aufgrund der veränderten Bedingungen draußen am Markt. Man muss heute im Marketing viel schneller reagieren, man muss dem Verkauf viel mehr Sachen an die Hand geben. Man muss auch viel stärker versuchen sich zu differenzieren und neue Wege zu gehen, wie z.B. durchs Medium Internet, oder einfach mal etwas machen, was niemand von einem erwartet, um sich weiterhin an der Spitze behaupten zu können.

Hiermit bestätige ich dieses Interview mir Frau Glaser am 11.03.2009 geführt zu habe.

B. Seebacher-Wolf

Brigitte Seebacher-Wolf)

Bibliography

Aaker, D. (1996), *Building Strong Brands*, 1. edt., New York 1996.

Aaker, D.; Joachimsthaler. E. (2000), *Brand Leadership*, 1. edt, New York 2000.

Aaker, J. (1997), Dimensions of Brand Personality, in: *Journal of Marketing Research*, Vol. XXXIV (August 1997), pp. 347-356.

Adlwarth, W. (1983), *Formen und bestimmungsgründe prestigegeleiteten Konsumentenverhaltens - Eine verhaltensempirische Analyse*, 1. edt., Münschen 1983.

Albright NYC (2009), under: http://www.albrightnyc.com (Status as of: 21.03.2009).

Atwal, G.; Williams, A. (2007), Experiencing luxury, in: *Admap*, March 2007, Issue 481, pp. 30-32.

Bag Borrow or Steal (2009), under: http://www.bagborroworsteal.com (Status as of: 21.03.2009).

Bearden, W.; Etzel, M. (1982), Reference Group Influence on Product and Brand Purchase Decisions, in: *Journal of Consumer Research*, Vol. 9, September 1982, pp. 183-194 .

Berry, C. (1994), *The Idea of Luxury: A Conceptual and Historical Investigation*, 1.edt., Cambridge 1994.

Birchall, J. (2007), *Die Angst des Luxus vor dem Internet*, in: FTD, under: http://www.ftd.de/karriere_management/management/:Die%20Angst%20Luxus%20Internet/190834.html (Status as of: 28.12.2008).

Birchall, J. (2008), *Luxury retailers hit by financial crisis while discounters' sales rise*, in: Financial Times, 9.10.2008, under: http://www.ft.com/cms/s/0/1b20a622-959b-11dd-aedd-000077b07658.html (Status as of: 14.02.2009).

Bruce, M.; Kratz, C. (2004), Competitive marketing strategies of luxury fashion companies, in: Hines, T.; Bruce, M. (Publisher), *Fashion Marketing. Contemporary issues*, 2. edt., Oxford et al. 2007.

Büttner, M.; Huber, F.; Regier, S.; Vollhardt, K. (2006), *Phänomen Luxusmarke. Identitätsstiftende Effekte und Determinanten der Markenloyalität*, 1. edt., Wiesbaden 2008.

Catry, B. (2003), The great pretenders: the magic of luxury goods, in: *Business Strategy Review*, Vol. 14, Issue 3, Autumn 2003, pp. 10-17.

Childers, T.; Rao, A. (1992), The influence of familial and peer-based reference groups on consumer decisions, in: *Journal of Consumer Research*, Vol. 19 No.2, pp. 198-211.

Cox, B. (2008), *Contemporary Luxury Perspectives. An Investigation for Consumption of Luxury Goods in Contemporary Society*, under: http://home.deds.nl/~bent/Thesis%20on%20luxury/Contemporary_Luxury_Perspectives_by_Ben_Cox.pdf (Status as of 3.03.2009).

Cp. Ricca, M. (2008), *The Luxury Kingdom*, under: http://www.interbrand.com/papers_list.aspx?langid=1000 (Status as of 28.03.2009).

Danzinger, P. (2005), *Let them eat cake. Marketing luxury to the masses - as well as the classes*, 1. edt., Chicago 2005.

David Report (2007), *Future Luxury*, under: http://davidreport.com/the-report/pdf/dr-200706/ (Status as of 30.03.2009).

Davies, L. (2008), *Chanel sheds 200 jobs as sales of luxury items decline*, in: The Guardian, 29.12.2008, under: htth://www.guardian.co.uk/business/2008/dec/29/chanel-job-cuts-bulgari-prada (Status as of: 14.02.2009).

De Barnier, V.; Rodina, I., Valette-Florence, P. (2006), *Which Luxury Perceptions Affect Most Consumer Purchase Behavior?: A Cross Cultural ExploratoryStudy in France, the United Kingdom and Russia,paper,* presented at The International Congress 'Marketing Trends', Università Ca' Foscari Venezia, Venice, Italy, 20–21 January 2006, under: http://www.escp-eap.net/conferences/marketing/2006_cp/Materiali/Paper/Fr/DeBarnier_Rodina_ValetteFlor ence.pdf (Status as of: 15.02.2009).

Dubois, B., Laurent, G., Czellar, S. (2001), *Consumer Rapport to Luxury: Analyzing Complex and Ambivalent Attitudes*, working paper 736, HEC, Jouy-en-Josas 2001.

Dubois, B.; Duquesne, P. (1993), The Market for Luxury Goods: Income versus Culture, in: *European Journal of Marketing*, Vol. 27 No.1, 2003 pp. 35-44.

Dubois, B.; Duquesne, P. (1993a), A new Approach to Identifying and Assessing Competitive Position - The Case of Luxury Brands, in: *Marketing and Research Today*, Vol. 21, Issue 2 (May), pp. 115-124.

Dubois, B.; Paternault, C. (1995), Observations: understanding the world of international luxury brands: the dream formula, in: *Journal of Advertising Research*, Vol. 35 No.4, pp.69-75

Dumoulin, D. (2007), What is today's definition of luxury, in: *Admap*, March 2007, Issue 481, pp. 27-29.

Feemers, M. (1992), *Der demonstrative aufwendige Konsum*, 1. edt., Frankfurt a. M. 1992.

Fisher, R.J. (1998), Group-derived consumption: the role of similarity and attractiveness in identification with a favourite sports team, in: *Advances in Consumer Research*, Vol. 25 No.1, pp. 283-288.

Fournier, S. (1998), Consumers and Their Brands: Developing Relationship Theory in Consumer Research, in: *Journal of Consumer Research*, Inc., Vol. 24, March 1998, pp. 343-373.

Groth, J. C. (1994), The exclusive value principle: a concept for marketing, in: *Journal of Product and Brand Management*, Vol. 3 No.3, pp.8-18.

Grugel-Pannier, D. (1996), *Luxus: Eine begriffs- und ideengeschichtliche Untersuchung unter besonderer Berücksichtigung von Bernhard Mandeville*, Frankfurt 1996.

Herrmann, A.; Huber, F.; Braunstein, C. (2005), Gestaltung der Markenpersönlichkeit mittels der means-end-Theorie, in: Esch, F.-R. (Publisher), *Moderene Markenführung*, 4. edt., Wiesbaden 2005, pp. 177-207.

Interbrand (2008), *The Leading Luxury Brands 2008*, under: http://www.interbrand.com/press_release.aspx?pressid=253&langid=1000 (Status as of: 22.12.2008).

Jurik, M. (2006), Zukunftsinstitut GmbH, *Der Neue Luxus*, translated by the author, under: http://www.zukunftsinstitut.de/downloads/rez_pm_Cash0406.pdf (Status as of: 18.02.2009).

Kambli, C.W. (1890), *Der Luxus nach seiner sittlichen und sozialen Bedeutung*, Frauenfeld 1890.

Kapferer, J.N. (1992), *Die Marke - Kapital des Unternehmens*, 1. edt., Augsburg 1992.

Kapferer, J.N. (1997), Managing Luxury Brands, in: *The Journal of Brand Management*, Vol. 4, No. 4, pp. 44-49.

Kapferer, J.N.; Bastien, V. (2009), *The Luxury Strategy. Break the Rules of Marketing to Build Luxury Brands*, 1. edt., London & Philadelphia 2009.

Kemper´s (2008), *Shopping auf Luxusmeilen*, under http://www.kempers-jll.net/index.php?spath=886&nav=meta&suche=luxusmeilen (Status as of: 27.03.2009)

Korneli, B. (2006), *Zur Problematik der internationalen Markenführung von Luxusmarken*, 1. edt., Hamburg 2006.

Krauss, C. (2008), *Worldwide luxury goods market growth projected to slow substantially by end of year and head into recession in 2009*, in: Bain and Company Press release, 29.10.2008, under: http://www.bain.com/bainweb/About/press_release_detail.asp?id=26657&menu_url=for_th e_media.asp (Status as of: 12.02.2009).

Lasslop, I. (2002), Identitätsorientierte Führung von Luxusmarken, in: Meffert, H.; Burmann, C.; Koers, M. (Publisher), *Markenmanagement: Grundfragen der identitätsorientierten Markenführung*, 2. edt., Wiesbaden, 2005, pp. 470-491.

Leibenstein (1966), Bandwagon-, Snob- und Veblen-Effekte in der Theorie der Konsumentennachfrage, in: Streissler, E.; Streissler, M. (Publisher), Konsum und Nachfrage, 1. edt., Köln et al. 1966, pp. 231-255.

Leibenstein, H. (1950), Bandwagon, Snob, and Veblen Effects in the Theory of Consumers´ Demand, in: *Quarterly Journal of Economics*, Vol. 44, pp. 183-207.

Lembke, J. (2009), *Der Luxusmarkt hat seinen Glanz verloren*, in FAZ 23.02.2009, Nr. 46, S. 20.

Levine, J. (2007), *Liberté, fraternité—but to hell with égalité!*, in: Forbes, 2.06.1997, under: http://www.forbes.com//forbes/97/0602/5911080a.html (Status as of 27.12.2008).

LVMH (2009), under: http://www.lvmh.com (Status as of: 21.02.2009).

Mandeville, B. (1988), *Die Bienenfabel*, 1. edt., Leipzig & München 1988.

Meffert, H./Burmann, C./Koers, M. (2005), *Markenmanagement Identitätsorientierte Markenführung und praktische Umsetzung*, 2. edt., Wiesbaden 2005.

Meffert, H/Burmann, C./Kirchgeorg, M. (2008), *Marketing - Grundlagen marktorientierter Unternehmensführung*, 10. edt., Wiesbaden 2008.

Mick, D.G.; DeMoss, M. (1990), Self-Gifts: Phenomenological Insights from Four Contexts, in: *Journal of Consumer Research*, Vol. 17 No.3, pp. 322- 332

Mila and Eddie (2009), under: http://www.milaandeddie.com.au (Status as of: 21.03.2009);

Moore, C. M.; Doherty, A.M. (2007), The international flagship stores of luxury fashion retailers, in: Hines, T.; Bruce, M. (Publisher), *Fashion Marketing. Contemporary issues*, 2. edt., Oxford et al. 2007.

N.N. (1969), *The American Heritage Dictionary of the English Language*, 4. edt., Boston 2000.

N.N. (2005), *China Becomes the World's Third Largest Consumer of Luxury Goods*, under: http://www.pressinterpreter.org/node/262 (Status as of: 27.03.2009).

N.N. (2007), *Das Designer ABC*, in: FAZ, 22.11.2007, under: http://www.faz.net/s/Rub789B86DE62AC40EBB47CE1E42725DCDC/Doc~E38655EE2D4 F14280BEA2FE47C6F4FA80~ATpl~Ecommon~Scontent.html (Status as of: 18.03.2009).

N.N. (2007,) *Die Textil- und Bekleidungsindustrie*, under: http://www.gesamttextil.de/deutsch/Die-Branche/K121.htm (Status as of: 13.03.2009).

Nia, A.; Zaichkowsky, J.L. (2000), Do counterfeits devalue the ownership of luxury brands?, in: *Journal of Product & Brand Management*, Vol. 9 No.7, pp. 485-497

Nueno, J.L.; Quelch, J.A. (1998), The mass marketing of luxury, in: *Business Horizons*, Vol. 4 No.5, pp. 61-68.

Okonkwo, U. (2007), *Luxury Fashion Branding-Trends, Tactics, Techniques*, 1. edt., New York 2007.

PPR (2009), under: http://www.ppr.com/front__sectionId-190_Changelang-en.html (Status as of: 21.02.2009)

Quintessentially (2009), under: http://www.quintessentially.com/home/ (Status as of: 24.03.2009).

Reich, C. (2005), *Faszinationskraft von Luxusmarken*, 1. edt., München & Mering 2005.

Renand, F.; Vickers,J. (2003), The Marketing of Luxury Goods: An exploratory study - three conceptual dimensions, in: *The Marketing Review*, Vol. 3, 2003, pp. 459-478.

Rosenberg, M. (1979), *Conceiving the Self*, 1. edt., New York 1979.

Roth, G. (2001), *Fühlen, Denken, Handel*, 1. edt., Frankfurt a.M. 2001.

Rozhon, T. (2004), *Luxury Market Blooms Near Red Square*, 17.09.2004, in: The New York Times, under:

http://www.nytimes.com/2004/09/17/business/worldbusiness/17luxury.html (Status as of: 04.04.2009).

Saller, S. (2004), Trading up: the democratisation of luxury, in: *The Market Leader*, Issue 25, Summer 2004, pp.16-17

Schmidt, D. (2007), *Die Mode der Gesellschaft. Eine systemtheoretische Analyse*, 1. edt, Baltmannsweiler 2007.

Silverstein, M.; Fiske, N. (2008), *Trading up. Why Consumers Want New Luxury Goods - and How Companies create them*, 3. edt., New York et al. 2008.

Simon, H.; Fassnacht, M. (2006), *Preismanagement: Analyse, Strategie, Umsetzung*, 3. edt., Wiesbaden 2006.

Sirgy, M. (1985), Using Self-Congruity and Ideal Congruity to Predict Purchase Motivation, in: *Journal of Business Research*, Vol. 13, pp.195-206.

Sirgy, M. et al. (1991), Self-congruity versus functional congruity: Predictors of consumer behavior, in: *Journal of the Academy of Marketing Science*, Vol.19 No. 4, pp. 363-375.

Sirgy, M. et al. (1997), Assessing the predictive validity of two methods of measuring self-image congruence, in: *Journal of the Academy of Marketing Science*, Vol. 25 No. 3, pp. 229-241.

Stegemann, N. (2006), Unique Brand Extension Challenges For Luxury Brands, in: *Journal of Business & Economics Research*, October 2006, Vol. 4 No. 10, pp. 57-68.

Thompson, J.C.; Engle, A.; Spain, J. (2005), *Counterfeit Products and Actor Proximity: An Exploratory Multidimensional Study Design*, under: http://people.eku.edu/englea/CounterfeitProdActorProx.pdf (Status as of 17.03.2009)

Trendwatching (2006), *Status Skills*, under: http://www.trendwatching.com/trends/status-skills.htm (Status as of: 23.03.2009).

Tsai, S. (2005), Impact of personal orientation on luxury-brand purchase value: an international investigation, in: *International Journal of Market Research*, Vol. 47, No. 4, 2005, pp.427-452

United Nations Interregional Crime and Justice Research Institute Report: *Counterfeiting: A Global Spread, A Global Threat*, under: http://www.unicri.it/news/1004-4_counterfeiting.php (Status as of: 20.03.2009).

Valtin, A. (2005), *Der Wert von Luxusmarken*, 1. edt., Wiesbaden 2005.

Veblen, T. (1899), *The Theory of the Leisure Class*, 1. edt., New York 1899.

Verdict Research (2007), *Global Luxury Retailing 2007*, under: http://www.verdict.co.uk/reports_european.htm (Status as of: 14.02.2009).

Viallon, P. (2006), Luxus zwischen Nachahnumg und Unerreichbarkeit. Eine kommunikative Annäherung an die Marketingstratgie, in: Boenigk, M.; Krieger, D.; Belliger, A.; Hug, C. (Publisher), *Innovative Wirtschaftskommunikation. Interdisziplinäre Problemlösungen für die Wirtschaft*, 1. edt., Wiesbaden, 2006, pp. 41-48.

Vigneron, F.; Johnson, L. (1999), A Review and a Conceptual Framework of Prestige-Seeking Consumer Behavior, in: *Academy of Marketing Science Review*, Vol. 9 No.1, pp.1-14.

Vigneron, F.; Johnson, L. (2004), Measuring perceptions of brand luxury, in: *Brand Management*, Vol. 11 No.6, pp. 484-506.

Weber, D. (2007), *Not Down and Out in Moscow*, 29.11.2007, in: The New York Times, under: http://www.nytimes.com/2007/11/29/fashion/29moscow.html (Status as of: 1.04.2009)

White, R. (2007), Marketing luxury - lapping up luxury, in: *Admap*, March 2007, Issue 481, pp. 19-20.

Wintour, A. in: Galliano, J. (2009), under: http://www.johngalliano.com (Status as of: 18.03.2009).

World Wealth Report 2008, Capgemini & Merrill Lynch, p.6, under: http://www.ml.com/media/100472.pdf (Status as of: 27.02.2009).

Yoon, C.; Gutchess, A.; Feinberg, F.; Polk, T. (2006), A Functional Magnetic Resonance Imaging Study of Neural Dissociations between Brand and Person Judgments, in: *Journal of Consumer Research*, Inc., Vol. 3.1, June 2, pp. 31-40.

Zalkin, C. (2008), *French Luxury Brands, A Modern Day Classic*, under: http://www.brandchannel.com/features_effect.asp?pf_id=413 (Status as of: 17.02.2009).

Lightning Source UK Ltd.
Milton Keynes UK
UKOW050633110112

185157UK00001B/136/P